MR. CHAIRMAN!

MR. CHAIRMAN !

*A Short Guide to the Conduct
and Procedure of Meetings*

WAL HANNINGTON

LAWRENCE AND WISHART LTD
LONDON

First published April 1950
Second impression June 1950
Reprinted 1955
Reprinted 1966
Reprinted 1975
Reprinted 1978

By the same author

THE RIGHTS OF ENGINEERS
INDUSTRIAL HISTORY IN WARTIME
UNEMPLOYED STRUGGLES, 1919–1936
BLACK COFFINS
SHORT HISTORY OF THE UNEMPLOYED
THE PROBLEM OF THE DISTRESSED AREAS
TEN LEAN YEARS

Printed and bound in Great Britain at
The Camelot Press Ltd, Southampton

CONTENTS

FOREWORD

THE PURPOSE of this small book is to explain the essential principles of Chairmanship and the rules for conducting business at trade union and public meetings.

Considering the millions of people within the trade union and political working-class movement today, and the fact that thousands of meetings have to be chaired in the course of a year, it is surprising that there are so few reference books dealing with this subject of Chairmanship.

Many workers have experienced a sense of fear and trepidation when called upon to "take the chair" because they suddenly realise that they are being called upon to undertake a position of responsibility without having the knowledge to enable them to do the job efficiently. Often they invent some excuse for declining the honour whilst inwardly wishing that they could accept. At such moments they probably regret not having a book on the subject of Chairmanship so that they could rise to the occasion.

But even amongst those who do not aspire to the office of Chairman, a knowledge of the rules of procedure is a valuable asset enabling them more intelligently to follow the business of the meeting and to participate in the proceedings instead of being merely passive listeners. It also enables them to assert their rights in the conduct of the meeting if the Chairman behaves in an undemocratic manner towards them.

The importance of a Chairman knowing his job cannot be too strongly emphasised. A Chairman who has a sound knowledge of the rules of debate can occupy his position with complete confidence and knows that he will receive the respect due to his office, even in a meeting where there is strong diversity of opinion.

A Chairman can make all the difference between a successful meeting and a failure. If he is a "good Chairman" he can steer the business through to a successful conclusion, whereas if he is a "bad Chairman", he can get himself and the meeting into a hopeless muddle.

Some people are more confident than others, but confidence alone is not sufficient to ensure the orderly conduct of a meeting. A Chairman must have a knowledge of the rules of procedure, otherwise he cannot conduct the business of a meeting efficiently. Confidence without knowledge borders on impudence and an audience will not be long in discovering that weakness.

In the case of trade union branch meetings, the

Chairman has a considerable influence not only upon the opinions of the members, but also on the extent of their attendance at the branch. An efficient Branch Chairman knows how to conduct the business in an interesting manner so that the members are encouraged to attend regularly. Therefore, every Branch Chairman should aim at becoming proficient in that office because, by doing so, he can render the maximum service to his union.

Some years ago I was asked to draft a small handbook for Branch Presidents. It was printed and issued, and many times in the course of my visits to Branches, I have heard unsolicited expressions of appreciation for the usefulness of that booklet.

This present publication is a more comprehensive survey on the subject of Chairmanship, covering not only trade union branch meetings but also various types of public meetings, committee meetings and conferences.

I trust it will serve the purpose for which it is written, namely, to extend the knowledge of Chairmanship and strengthen the general working-class movement.

WAL HANNINGTON

December 1949.

PART I

SOME PRELIMINARIES

THE TITLE of this little book was chosen to emphasise the fact that from the moment that a meeting opens, whether public or private, to the time that it closes, the Chairman has the responsibility for seeing that it is conducted in an orderly and business-like manner. He does so by guiding the proceedings in accordance with certain established rules, through which he controls the meeting and ensures that the business is dealt with efficiently.

These *Rules of Debate,* as they are called, have not been established by any legal enactment, they have evolved out of common practice and have been defined from time to time by various organisations and business institutions with the result that we have a commonly accepted code of procedure for the management of meetings (see pp. 31-39).

In principle, the rules for dealing with motions and amendments arising from any meeting are the same, but the procedure for conducting the meeting varies according to the nature of the meeting. For instance, a trade union branch meeting, a public meeting and a delegate conference are three entirely different assemblies and require a different procedure for transacting their business. Whilst the procedure in each case necessarily differs, there is, in the main, a common practice in respect of each type of assembly.

STANDING ORDERS

ESTABLISHED organisations and committees usually have their own *Standing Orders* for the regulation of their business meetings. Standing Orders is in fact a set of rules which lay down a specific procedure for the meetings of that organisation or committee and which amplify the common Rules of Debate.

Standing Orders usually cover such questions as: the time of opening and closing the meeting; the order in which the business shall be dealt with; the duties of the Chairman and Secretary in regard to the meeting; what constitutes a quorum, i.e., the number or proportion of members who must be present to constitute a meeting and give validity to its proceedings; the method of submitting motions to the meeting; the time limit for speakers in discussion, the method for voting and the procedure for challenging the vote; the rights of the Chairman and

Secretary in voting; and the proportion of majority votes required to carry a motion.

When Standing Orders touch upon the commonly accepted Rules of Debate, the Standing Orders are the rules which must be abided by in that meeting. Therefore, it is most essential that the Chairman, in addition to having a sound knowledge of the general Rules of Debate, should be fully conversant with the Standing Orders of his own organisation, otherwise he may be challenged on procedure by some sharp member of the meeting who knows the Standing Orders.

It is possible, however, to depart from the Standing Orders providing the meeting agrees. The Standing Orders usually contain a rule which makes provision for their suspension. For instance, in the course of business, the meeting might desire to have some urgent matter raised, which is not provided for on the agenda; or, in the course of discussion, it might desire that the time allowed for speeches should be extended; or, it might desire to continue the meeting beyond the specified closing time. In such circumstances, the procedure should be that somebody formally moves the suspension of Standing Orders, the Chairman submits that motion to a vote and, if it is carried by a majority, the Chairman permits the departure from Standing Orders.

Strictly speaking, when suspension of Standing Orders is moved, the mover should name the particular rule which he wants suspended because his motion is not really intended to suspend the whole of the Standing Orders but only that portion which at the moment is an impediment to the meeting. It is therefore advisable for the rules making up the Standing Orders to be numbered so as to facilitate the suspension of any one rule. Even so, such precise suspension is usually only possible in committee meetings where all those present are fully conversant with the Standing Orders. In larger meetings, such as a trade union branch, the general practice is simply to move "suspension of Standing Orders". In such cases the Chairman should indicate to the meeting the particular rule which he assumes the mover is referring to and this should be done before he takes the vote so that the meeting knows exactly what it is voting on. In taking the vote for suspension of Standing Orders the common practice is that such a motion must have at least a two-thirds majority in favour to be declared carried. A bare majority is not regarded as authoritative enough to suspend Standing Orders.

The suspension of Standing Orders must not be allowed to develop into a practice otherwise there is little value in having Standing Orders at all. The

Chairman must guard against any abuse of the right to suspend Standing Orders and he should exercise his authority against suspension and express his opposition to it if he thinks strongly that suspension is not necessary. Where Standing Orders contain a rule to the effect that the Chairman's ruling on any point of order or procedure is final and binding upon the meeting, he has complete authority to reject a motion for suspension of Standing Orders. A good Chairman, however, will always avoid acting in a dictatorial manner except in most extreme circumstances. It should be the aim of a good Chairman to carry the meeting with him in support of his ruling rather than enforce his powers.

CHALLENGING THE CHAIRMAN

IN A democratic meeting each person making up the audience has certain rights in regard to its conduct. The Chairman is entitled to co-operation from his audience in the carrying out of his duties, but he is not entitled to expect the audience to passively tolerate arrogance or unfair procedure on his part.

The Chairman's ruling should not be accepted as final if it is contrary to established procedure or is unreasonable and against the general wishes of the meeting. The Chairman is there to guide the meeting, not to boss it. He has specific powers by virtue of his office but he must not be allowed to abuse those powers by behaving in an undemocratic manner towards his audience.

If he does so, any member of the audience has the right to challenge his ruling or his general handling of the meeting. The person who does so must rise to his feet and say, *"Mr. Chairman, I want to challenge your ruling,"* or, *"I wish to challenge the way in which you are conducting this meeting."*

When such a challenge is made, if there are others in the meeting who indicate that they support it, the Chairman must accept the challenge and test the feeling of the meeting. Standing Orders sometimes define the conditions for carrying out such a challenge by laying down the number of persons who must indicate their support before the Chairman accepts it. In that case immediately the challenge is made, the Chairman must ask if the requisite number of supporters are present (it might be four or more), and if they do not respond he can over-rule the challenge.

But if the required number do respond he must accept it and the Challenger then has the right to state his grounds of objection, and the Chairman has the right to reply and defend his actions.

When such a challenge is made it is the usual procedure for the Chairman, after accepting it, to

16

temporarily vacate the Chair and hand the proceedings over to the Secretary or some other official in the meeting until the issue has been decided. No discussion is allowed on a challenge to a Chairman's ruling beyond the statement of the Challenger and the reply of the Chairman. The matter must then be put to the vote of the meeting by show of hands, in the following form, "*All those in favour of upholding the Chairman's ruling,*" and then, "*All those against*". If the majority of the votes are against the Chairman, he must accept that decision and conform to it in his ruling.

If the Standing Orders do not lay down any specific number of supporters to make the challenge valid, the Challenger only requires to find a seconder, and the Chairman must accept it.

It may happen that the conduct of the Chairman in general is so objectionable that the audience wish to do more than simply challenge his ruling on some point. In that case a much more drastic line might be taken. Unless the rules of the organisation or the Standing Orders protect him the Chairman might be removed from the Chair. This can be done by somebody formally moving a motion, "*That the Chairman leaves the Chair,*" or, "*That this meeting has no confidence in the Chairman.*"

Such a motion must find a seconder before it can

be accepted and then the Chairman must temporarily retire from the Chair whilst it is debated. This is something much more serious in its effects than a challenge to a Chairman's ruling and therefore such a motion should be made the subject of a full discussion in which everybody has the right to express an opinion vocally before they are called upon to vote. The Chairman must have the right to speak in reply to his critics before the vote is taken.

If the motion is defeated the Chairman should regard it as a vote of confidence in himself and resume his position in the Chair. But if the motion is carried the Chairman must take it as the democratic will of the meeting and accept his defeat. In cases where the Standing Orders make provision for such a procedure a two-thirds majority is usually required to carry such a motion. But even where the Standing Orders do not lay down such a provision it is advisable on a drastic motion of this nature to apply the two-thirds majority rule, as this leaves no doubt about the will of the meeting. A bare majority would not be a convincing decision on such a drastic step as removing the Chairman, and would probably provoke prolonged controversy and counter-moves by the minority. A two-thirds majority would be an overwhelming decision which could not be challenged.

Following the decision to remove the Chairman the officer who is temporarily presiding must then ask the meeting for nominations for a new Chairman and proceed with the election in the usual way. If it is a meeting of an established organisation he will, of course, be bound to proceed in accordance with the rules governing such an election.

Although an audience has the right to deal with a Chairman who forfeits their respect, they must not allow this right to be abused by individuals frivolously challenging the Chair and thereby obstructing the normal business of the meeting.

THE CHAIRMAN WHO ARRIVES LATE

THE MEETING cannot commence without a Chairman and it is most essential that he should be punctual in his attendance. A Chairman who frequently arrives late not only injures his own prestige, but he also encourages those who attend the meeting to fall into the bad practice of arriving late. It can result in the position where the Chairman, when he does arrive on time, has to sit waiting for a quorum before he can "take the Chair" and consequently the time for transacting business is reduced.

A Chairman who is prompt in attendance is in a very strong position to rebuke those persons who make a practice of arriving late and who, when the meeting is reaching the specified closing time, move suspension of Standing Orders for the purpose of extending the time of the meeting. The Chairman who also comes late is not in the position to do this.

When the meeting assembles on time and the Chairman is late, those present sometimes decide formally to appoint one of their number to occupy the Chair temporarily so that the meeting can begin. In such a situation, when the official Chairman does arrive, he should quietly take a seat and wait until the item under discussion is cleared before he approaches the Chairman's table to take over his duties. This is not only the most dignified thing to do in the circumstances, but it shows due respect towards the person who stepped into the breach. In fact, the Chairman who arrives after the meeting has opened and proceeds immediately to remove the other person from the Chair in the middle of a discussion, adds to his first offence of late arrival by abruptly interrupting the proceedings and by displaying an ungainly lack of elementary courtesy towards the temporary Chairman and the audience. Such a person should not be surprised if the temporary Chairman makes him feel very small by asserting his right to finish the item under discussion before he hands over "the Chair".

PREPARATION FOR THE MEETING

IT IS not only essential for the Chairman to be there for the opening of the meeting, but it is advisable for him to be in attendance a little earlier so that he has time to acquaint himself with the business which is to be dealt with. This applies to any meeting and especially to a trade union branch where various items are on the agenda, such as: correspondence, reports, announcement notices, ballots for election of officers, invitations for delegates to local conferences, etc.

A Chairman who peruses his material before opening the meeting can handle it much more efficiently during the proceedings than one who has not done so. We have all seen the Chairman who bores the meeting with his hesitations and misquotations in the reading of correspondence and documents because he has not troubled previously to read them. What a jarring effect that has on the minds of the listeners! We have also seen the Chairman who tries to make good his omissions by studying the next item of business whilst the previous one is under discussion, with the result that he is not listening to what is being said and at some vital moment, when he should be fully alert, he is in a mental haze and takes several moments to recover his control of the proceedings. These examples of inefficient Chairmanship show

how necessary it is for the Chairman to acquaint himself with the business before the meeting opens. To do so implies that the Secretary must also be in attendance before the meeting opens so that he can pass the agenda and necessary documents to the Chairman and consult with him on any doubtful point.

Before the Chairman opens the meeting he should sort the various documents into their agenda order so that he doesn't have to search for them whilst the meeting is in progress. The meeting should not begin casually, it should be opened in a business-like manner by the Chairman rising to his feet, using his gavel or bell to call for order and formally announcing "I declare this meeting open."

AGENDA AND TIME-TABLE

AN AGENDA is always necessary at a meeting. It sets out for the guidance of the Chairman the item or items which are to be dealt with by the meeting. It is always advisable for the agenda to be compiled on the basis of a time-table so that provision can be made for all items to be dealt with before the closing time of the meeting. Even at a meeting where there is only one item on the agenda a time-table is necessary if there are to be questions and discussions. In that case a specified time is laid down for the speaker and likewise for the questions and discussion.

At trade union branches or other meetings where numerous items are on the agenda, a time-table is essential, otherwise undue time can be taken up on minor matters to the exclusion of more important business. It is precisely in the steering of the meeting in a manner which ensures that all the business is adequately dealt with within the allotted time that the qualities of the Chairman are tested and revealed. A capable Chairman is able to estimate the business before him and the time necessary for each item. If there is more business than the meeting time will properly allow for, he must take responsibility for eliminating matter which is least urgent and can be left out. It it much better to do this than to deal inadequately with the more important business.

During the proceedings the Chairman should aim at conserving time, and if he can keep a little ahead of his time-table, it will provide him with a latitude to cope with unexpected incidents in subsequent items. It is the duty of the Chairman to prevent waste of time, and when he feels that any item under discussion has been adequately dealt with, he should propose to the meeting the closure of that business, and with approval, pass on to the next item on the agenda.

It frequently happens that an item of correspondence leads to a discussion without a formal motion being before the meeting. In the course of the discussion it becomes evident that the meeting wishes to record a decision. The Chairman should then ask for a motion so that the discussion becomes explicit instead of general. This usually hastens the conclusion and prevents waste of time.

Even the best of Chairmen sometimes finds it difficult to adhere strictly to the time-table when a keen controversy arises on some item of business. In such circumstances he can suggest a limit to the number of speakers and a reduced limit to the length of speeches. He can usually carry the meeting with him on such a proposal if he points out that such a course is necessary to enable him to get through the agenda. If, with this course of action, he is still behind his time-table, he will have to make adjustments on subsequent items or decide in accordance with circumstances either to eliminate certain items or ask the meeting to agree to an extension of time.

If he decides on the course of eliminating certain items, he should announce his intention and ask the meeting for formal approval. If the meeting does not wish those items to be eliminated, it can then propose the alternative course of extending the time of the meeting. If there is a division of opinion in the meeting on whether the closing time should be extended, the Chairman should take a vote "for" and "against". If there is no Standing Order which governs this, the Chairman should rule that a bare majority is not sufficient to justify an extension of time but that the will of the meeting should be decisively expressed by at least a two-thirds majority. Unless he does this he may find himself with only half a meeting during the extension period which may give rise to doubts about the validity of any decisions which are taken during that period. A two-thirds majority present would not be questioned.

If the principle of extension is agreed to, the meeting should decide the limit of the extension. This is most important, otherwise the proceedings can drag on indefinitely, with people leaving all the time thereby causing a very unsatisfactory ending to the meeting. For the very reason that any extension of time usually means that some people leave before the end of the meeting, it is desirable that the Chairman should endeavour to conduct the business in a manner that will make extension of time unnecessary.

At statutory meetings, e.g. trade union branches, the Chairman should firmly endeavour to prevent extension of time becoming a regular practice. It causes discontent amongst members who find that they have to leave before the business is concluded and it can have the effect of discouraging attendance.

PART II

TERMS, RULES AND PROCEDURE

TERMS USED FOR TRANSACTING BUSINESS

IT IS absolutely essential for the Chairman to know the terms used, and their meaning, in respect to the procedure for transacting business at a meeting. Those most commonly in use are: MOTIONS, SUB-STANTIVE MOTIONS, RESOLUTIONS, DIRECT NEGATIVE, AMENDMENTS, REFERENCE BACK, ADDENDUMS, THE QUESTION BE PUT, RIDERS, PREVIOUS QUESTION, POINTS OF ORDER, NEXT BUSINESS.

Before explaining these terms it is worth while noting an error that has become so common as almost to be an established practice in the trade union and labour movement. Usually it will be found that the Chairman calls upon the meeting to vote on the *Resolution* under discussion, whereas to be strictly correct he should speak of the *Motion*, because the term Resolution only applies *after* the Motion has been voted on and carried.

But this is purely a technical point and from the standpoint of conducting an ordinary working-class meeting it does not really matter which term is used. Later on, when we come to consider the procedure for moving, discussing and voting on Motions (see pp. 39-43), we shall keep to the correct term, but if a Chairman prefers to use the term Resolution, instead of Motion there is no strong reason why he should not do so, as long as it does not cause any confusion as to the meaning amongst those who are being asked to vote.

MOTION

A *Motion* is a proposition submitted for discussion and vote. It must be positive in its wording and declare an opinion or call for a course of action—or both.

RESOLUTION

A *Resolution* is a Motion which has been put to the vote and carried.

AMENDMENT

When a Motion is before the meeting an *Amendment* is a proposition to change the words of the Motion as a whole, or to change certain words, or to add or delete words anywhere in the Motion.

27

ADDENDUM

An *Addendum* is a proposition to add words at the end of the Motion.

RIDER

A *Rider* is similar to an Addendum in so far that it seeks to add words at the end of the Motion. But whereas in the case of the Addendum, words added become an integral part of the Motion, the Rider is usually in the form of a suggestion or recommendation related to the carrying out of the principle contained in the Motion.

POINT OF ORDER

A *Point of Order* is an objection raised by a member of the audience on the grounds that a speaker is departing from the subject under discussion, or that the Standing Orders are not being observed, or that the recognised rules of debate are not being operated, or that the speaker is using offensive language.

SUBSTANTIVE MOTION

When an Amendment is voted on and carried by a majority it replaces or alters the original Motion and then becomes known as the *Substantive Motion*, to which new Amendments can be moved, providing they are not the same in wording or principle as that in the original Motion which was lost.

DIRECT NEGATIVE

A *Direct Negative* is a proposed amendment to a Motion which offers no alternative proposition but simply seeks to negate the whole Motion. A Direct Negative must therefore always be ruled out of order by the Chairman, since its purpose can be achieved simply by voting against the Motion; and it is thus unnecessary.

REFERENCE BACK

Reference Back is a proposition against a report which is under discussion, and may refer to the whole report or a section of it. It means that the meeting does not approve of the report, and wishes the committee which was responsible for drafting it, to alter it in accordance with the objection specified by the mover of the Reference Back.

THE QUESTION BE PUT

To move *that the question be now put,* means that the discussion should cease and the vote should be taken on the Motion (or Amendment if any) which is before the meeting.

PREVIOUS QUESTION

Moving *the Previous Question* means that no vote should be taken on the original Motion which is before the meeting. If the Previous Question is carried it therefore dismisses the original Motion without a vote, but if the Previous Question is not carried it means that the Chairman without any further discussion must proceed to take the vote on the original Motion. The effect therefore of moving the Previous Question is to close the discussion on the original question whether the Previous Question is carried or lost.

NEXT BUSINESS

Moving *Next Business* means that the meeting should immediately proceed to the next item of business. It can be moved at any time in reference to any item on the agenda, but if it is moved and carried whilst a Motion or an Amendment is under discussion it dismisses the Motion and Amendment without any vote being taken on them. In this respect it is the same as the Previous Question, but if Next Business is not carried, then the meeting resumes discussion on the original Motion and Amendment, and thereafter takes the vote on them in the usual way.

RULES OF DEBATE

A CHAIRMAN must have a knowledge of the *Rules of Debate,* otherwise he cannot efficiently control discussions on Motions and Amendments, etc. This knowledge is especially necessary when the discussion becomes highly controversial and numerous propositions are moved.

Except where Standing Orders state to the contrary, the following rules affecting the rights of speech are those which operate in general practice at all ordinary meetings.

All persons moving and seconding Motions and Amendments, etc., and all those who participate in the discussion, must do so standing. The speaker then "has the floor". The only exception to this rule is in committee meetings. Of course if the speaker is physically disabled and unable to stand with ease the Chairman can give him permission to address the meeting without rising to his feet.

A speaker must address his remarks to the Chairman and not to any individual member of the audience even though he may be replying to the previous remarks of an individual.

The mover of a Motion has the right to speak when introducing his Motion and the right to reply to the discussion as the last speaker, before the vote is taken.

If there is nobody willing to second the Motion after it has been moved, the Motion falls, which means that no discussion can be permitted on it, and the Chairman must pass to next business.

The seconder of a Motion has the right to speak when seconding but, unlike the mover, he has no right of reply. If he formally seconds the Motion without speaking he has the right to speak during the discussion on it, but he cannot speak twice.

If, during the discussion, the mover wishes to withdraw his Motion, he cannot do so without the consent of the seconder and the meeting. If there is an Amendment before the meeting he must also obtain the consent of the mover and seconder of the Amendment before he can withdraw his Motion. If they object, the Motion remains for debate and vote.

The mover of an Amendment has the right to speak only when introducing it. He has no right of reply to the discussion.

Those who take part in discussion on a Motion are only permitted to speak once. But if, after they have spoken, an Amendment is moved to the Motion, they are entitled to speak again on the Amendment. If the Amendment has been moved before they speak they can only speak once.

Any one who has already spoken on the original Motion loses his right to move or second an Amendment to that Motion. But if the Motion is afterwards amended he may then speak again and move a further Amendment.

The mover of an Amendment which is carried and becomes the Substantive Motion has no right of reply, but if a further Amendment is moved, he has the right, in common with others, to speak on that Amendment.

The mover and seconder of an unsuccessful Amendment have no right to move another Amendment dealing with the same point in the Motion, but they have the right to move another Amendment to some other paragraph in the Motion.

The mover or seconder of a Motion which is afterwards amended has the right to move a further Amendment to the Substantive Motion, providing that it does not raise a principle which has already been defeated.

Addenda and Riders to motions must be moved and seconded in the same manner as Amendments, but as they are additions to the Motion and not in opposition to it, the mover and seconder of the Motion can agree to accept the Addendum or Rider as an addition to their Motion. But this acceptance can only be made with the general approval of the meeting. It can happen that the Addendum or Rider proposes something which is controversial.

In that event the Chairman must rule that it be dealt with in the same manner as an Amendment, namely, as a separate proposition to the Motion.

It is permissible for any one who has not spoken in the debate to test the feeling of the meeting on whether the debate should close, by moving "that the question be put". Those who have already spoken are not entitled to move this. The Motion, "that the question be put," takes precedence over the original Motion. It must be formally seconded before it is in order, and then it must be submitted immediately to the vote of the meeting. If it is carried, the Chairman must then declare the discussion closed and call upon the mover of the original Motion to make his reply to the discussion which has taken place, and thereafter take the vote on the original Motion. If the Motion "that the question be put" is defeated, the meeting resumes discussion where it left off.

If, in addition to the original Motion, there is an Amendment before the meeting, the person who moves "that the question be put" should make it clear whether his Motion applies only to the Amendment or to both Amendment and original Motion. If it applies only to the Amendment and is carried, the Chairman must then ask the mover of the original Motion if he wishes to reply before he takes the vote on the Amendment. If the Amendment is defeated, that leaves the original Motion still standing and open for further discussion and for new Amendments.

If the mover of the original Motion has made his reply to discussion on the direct Amendment he is not entitled to a second reply on a subsequent Amendment, but he is entitled to speak again, the same as others, in the debate on such further Amendment.

A person who moves an unsuccessful Motion "that the question be put" loses his right to speak on the original Motion or Amendment when the discussion is resumed. The same rule applies to anybody who moves an unsuccessful Motion for Next Business.

It is quite "in order" for someone to move "that the question be put" whilst a speaker is addressing the meeting and the speaker must then immediately resume his seat whilst the vote is taken on that Motion. This interruption of a speaker, although in order, is not a desirable practice, because it is discourteous and can result in bad feeling being created. If the Motion "that the question be put" is defeated, the interrupted speaker has the right to resume the discussion where he was stopped.

During discussion on a Motion or Amendment, a person who has not already spoken can move Next Business. This is a more drastic method of closing the debate, because if it is carried it dismisses the original Motion and Amendment without a vote. If it is lost, the debate is resumed, but the mover of Next Business has no right to participate in it. A Motion for Next Business cannot be accepted unless it is seconded. The Next Business cannot be moved whilst a speaker is on his feet.

Because of the drastic nature of Next Business, the Chairman, if he thinks that everybody in the meeting is not clear on the meaning of this Motion, can make it clear before he takes the vote. There is no rule that he should do so, but it is desirable that he should, otherwise some people might vote for Next Business without understanding that the carrying of this automatically dismisses the original Motion and Amendment.

A still more drastic and confusing Motion is the *Previous Question*. The effect of this Motion, if carried, is to dismiss the original Motion without a vote being taken on it, whilst if lost, it rules out any further discussion and compels the Chairman to immediately take the vote on the original Motion. The Previous Question cannot be moved when there is an Amendment before the meeting, because the Previous Question is itself an Amendment to the original Motion. If there are Amendments on the agenda which have not yet been moved, the Previous

Question can be moved, but the effect of it being carried is to dismiss not only the original Motion but also the intended Amendments.

Because of the drastic character of the Previous Question and the fact that it could so easily be abused to stifle discussion, the Chairman has the right to refuse to accept such a Motion unless it appears to be in accordance with the general wishes of the meeting. The Previous Question is so often a confusing Motion to a general audience, that it is not advisable to encourage the use of it.

A Point of Order can be raised at any moment during a debate on a Motion or when some subject is being discussed without a Motion. It can even be raised when a vote is being taken on a Motion. It must be related to the conduct or procedure of the meeting, such as a violation of the Standing Orders or rules of the organisation; an infringement of the rules of debate; a speaker departing from the subject under discussion and introducing irrelevancies; indulging in offensive language; or a challenge about the voting procedure. The person who raises a Point of Order is really calling for the Chairman's ruling on the point and therefore he should put it in question form to the Chairman. He must rise to his feet and say, "A point of order, Mr. Chairman." The Chairman must then request the person who was interrupted to immediately resume his seat whilst the Point of Order is stated and the ruling is being given. A Point of Order must be very brief and to the point. It must not take the form of a statement. Further, a person is not entitled to call a Point of Order simply because he disagrees with the opinion of the speaker. If the debate is being conducted with a time limit on the speakers, extra time must be allowed to a speaker who is interrupted by a Point of Order.

Within the category of Points of Order there are two other points on which the proceedings of the meeting can be interrupted namely, a *Point of Explanation* and a *Point of Information.*

An opponent might deliberately distort or misquote the remarks of a previous speaker or it may be a genuine misunderstanding of what was said or meant. In such a case the speaker who is being misquoted has the right to rise on a Point of Explanation and ask the Chairman's permission to correct the misrepresentation. The granting of a Point of Explanation by the Chairman does not entitle the speaker to indulge in a controversial argument, he must make a brief, straightforward explanation of the point and resume his seat. A Point of Explanation can be raised whilst the offending speaker is addressing the meeting.

Sometimes a member of the audience simply wants information relative to the procedure or the subject under discussion. In that case he is entitled to rise on a Point of Information but he is not entitled to do so whilst somebody else is speaking. He must wait until the speaker has finished and catch the eye of the Chairman before the next speaker begins.

The Point of Order is a practice which calls for firmness on the part of the Chairman, because if it is allowed to be abused it can have a very disturbing effect upon the conduct of the meeting and can reduce the authority and control of the Chairman. Therefore, the Chairman must guard against this abuse and firmly rebuke any person who irresponsibly or frivolously jumps up on Points of Order. The provision for Points of Order is not there to facilitate disorder.

The Chairman is the controller of the meeting and when he rises to his feet he "has the floor". Even if someone else is speaking at the time, that person must immediately resume his seat until called upon by the Chairman to continue his remarks.

PROCEDURE FOR DISCUSSION OF MOTIONS, ETC.

THE PROCEDURE for moving a Motion is that the mover must rise to his feet and say *"Mr. Chairman,*

I wish to move the following Motion." He then reads his Motion to the meeting or formulates it orally. It is advisable that the Motion be put in writing by the mover before it is proposed, especially if it exceeds a dozen words in length and cannot be easily remembered by those in the meeting.

But in most cases in trade union branch meetings, Motions are not submitted in writing at the moment they are moved because often they are not premeditated but arise out of a general discussion on some matter before the branch.

In such cases the proposer of a Motion formulates it orally. If it is a very short Motion and the exact words can easily be recorded by the Chairman or the Minute Secretary, there is no need for the mover to write it out. For instance a Motion, *"That we send delegates to the Trades Council Conference,"* does not require to be submitted in writing by the mover.

If, however, the Motion is longer and more involved it might be moved orally, but in such cases the practice is for the Chairman to request the mover to write it out whilst the discussion is proceeding so that he has the exact words of the Motion before him when he submits it to the vote.

After formulating his Motion orally or reading it to the meeting, the mover states his reasons for proposing the Motion and then sits down. Before anyone else speaks the Chairman must ask if there is a seconder for the Motion. If nobody is prepared to second it the Motion falls and the Chairman proceeds to the next item of business. No discussion, other than the opening speech of the mover, can be allowed on a Motion which is not seconded, because in effect no seconder means that nobody else in the meeting supports it.

It is not necessary for a seconder to speak in support when seconding. He can say *"I formally second the Motion, Mr. Chairman,"* and that puts it in order for discussion. By formally seconding the Motion he reserves his right to speak later during the discussion. This is a method which is often used when the seconder expects opposition to the Motion, because it enables him to answer the opponents in discussion. There is, however, a danger in this method, because if the seconder waits too long, somebody may move that The Question be Put, or, Next Business, and if carried, that would debar the seconder from speaking. Therefore if he is reserving his right to speak he must carefully estimate the feeling of the meeting and rise to speak before a closure Motion is moved.

When a Motion has been moved orally and the Chairman requests it in writing, the mover should attend to this immediately after he has spoken and pass it up to the Chairman. In order to make the terms of the Motion quite clear to the meeting and to facilitate the moving of Amendments, the Chairman can read the Motion again even after the discussion has started.

Those wishing to participate in discussion must rise to their feet immediately the previous speaker sits down. The Chairman must be impartial and fair in naming the next speaker and if two persons rise to their feet at the same time he must indicate which one is to speak and give preference to the other one over those who may rise later. (In Conferences, however, the procedure is often different from an ordinary Meeting and this will be explained later under the heading of Conferences, see pp. 134-136.)

If in the course of the discussion the Chairman finds that several speakers follow each other, all supporting the Motion or all opposing it, he should ask for a speaker who wishes to put the contrary point of view, and so endeavour to get speakers "for" and "against" the Motion to speak alternately. If there are no speakers to the contrary it can often be regarded as an indication that the meeting has already made up its mind on how it will vote, and the Chairman can then suggest that the Motion be put to the vote so that unnecessary time on discussion can be prevented.

After the mover of the Motion has been given the opportunity of replying to the discussion the Chairman should again read the Motion to the meeting before taking the vote. No further discussion can be allowed. He then proceeds to take the vote. If the method is by show of hands he should say "*All those in favour of the Motion, please show.*" Having counted the show of hands and noted the number, the Chairman says "*All those against the Motion, please show.*" After counting those votes, he declares the Motion carried or lost, accordingly. It is important to note that the affirmative vote on the Motion must be taken first, and the negative second.

MOVING AMENDMENTS

After a Motion has been moved and seconded it is open to anybody in the meeting to move an Amendment. Like the Motion, the Amendment must find a seconder otherwise it cannot be accepted by the Chairman.

Movers and seconders of Amendments have the right to speak to the Amendment but unlike the mover of the Motion, the mover of the Amendment has no right of reply at the end of discussion.

An Amendment can be moved directly following the moving and seconding of the Motion, or it can be moved at any time during the discussion on the

Motion. But it is better for it to be moved as soon as possible after the Motion so that the discussion can centre around the two propositions.

An Amendment may seek to substitute the words of the Motion as a whole, or to substitute certain words, or to simply add or delete words in the Motion. So now let us consider some examples of Motions and Amendments.

For instance, the Motion might be:

"That this meeting has considered the information supplied by our Union Executive on the profits taken by the employers in our industry over the past year, and strongly protests at these high profits at a time when our wages are so low. We call upon our Executive to organise a national publicity campaign to expose these profits and to build up public opinion in support of our claim for higher wages. The campaign should include the organising of demonstrations in all the industrial towns on Sunday, August 3. In the event of the employers rejecting our claim for a wage increase we call upon the Union Executive to take a national strike ballot of the membership."

The foregoing is an example of a highly controversial Motion to which various Amendments might be moved as follows:

"Delete all words after the first paragraph ending 'so low', and substitute, 'We therefore call upon the

Government to take the necessary action to prohibit any employer from taking profits in excess of ten per cent'."

Such an Amendment, if carried, would defeat that portion of the Motion which proposes a national publicity campaign, demonstrations in all the towns, and the taking of a strike ballot.

Another Amendment might simply be opposed to the date of the demonstrations because the mover thinks that more time for preparation is needed. His Amendment might therefore be:

"Delete Sunday, August 3 and substitute September 7."

Again, somebody might agree with all the Motion except the point calling for a strike ballot. He would then move:

"Delete all words in the last paragraph after 'Union Executive' and substitute, 'to pursue the claim through national arbitration procedure'."

From the foregoing it will be seen that these Amendments are all different in their purpose yet none of them oppose the Motion as a whole. They all aim at the deletion of certain proposals in the Motion and the substitution of alternative proposals.

OMNIBUS MOTION

A Motion such as the one stated above, which

contains several clauses each dealing with related, but separate, proposals, is known as an *Omnibus Motion*. Such a Motion provides the basis for more than one Amendment, as the above examples show.

Only one Amendment can be proposed and discussed at a time and this must be voted on before another Amendment is moved. In the case of an Omnibus Motion which is likely to provoke more than one Amendment, the Chairman on receiving the first Amendment should ask if there are any further Amendments. If there are, he should take these as notice of further Amendments and before discussion takes place on the first Amendment he should read to the meeting the subsequent Amendments which are proposed. There are two very good reasons for doing this, first, to acquaint the meeting with the alternatives which are being proposed so that these are in mind when the vote is taken on the first Amendment, and secondly, to enable him to submit the Amendments in their proper order of paragraph sequence to the Motion.

In strict procedure he should not take an Amendment dealing with the last paragraph of the Motion and then allow one to follow dealing with the first paragraph. When there are several Amendments they should be taken in the order in which the clauses to be amended appear in the Motion.

Therefore in the case where several Amendments are notified, the Chairman should not necessarily take the Amendments in the order of notification. If the last Amendment to be notified deals with an earlier portion of the Motion he should take that Amendment first.

This is a situation which really calls for alert and clear-minded Chairmanship. He must be able to see the implications involved in the various Amendments and handle them in such a way as not to cause confusion in the meeting.

When there are several Amendments it is not always a simple matter of taking them in the order mentioned above, because some may cover more than one clause in the Motion.

For instance, look again at the first example Amendment. The effect of that Amendment, if carried, would be to rule out the two following Amendments because it would delete all clauses of the Motion after the first clause, thereby invalidating the other Amendments.

If he took the second Amendment first it would, if carried, put the first Amendment out of order because the meeting has already decided in favour of demonstrations on September 7. Likewise if he took the third Amendment first and it was carried, it would invalidate the first Amendment because the meeting has already decided to ask the Union Executive to take the wage claim to arbitration.

Therefore, in the examples of Amendments stated above, they have been set out in the proper order in which they should be taken, and if the first Amendment had been notified to the Chairman last, he should nevertheless bring that Amendment forward as the first. But it often happens that after an Amendment to a latter clause of the Motion has been moved, discussed and voted on, somebody thinks of another Amendment to an earlier clause. Although it is not strict procedure for the Chairman to accept this, he should, however, exercise his judgment and if it does not run contrary to a principle already decided he may accept it. But he must be on his guard about doing so lest he opens the door to a succession of such Amendments which can easily lead to confusion. He must use his Chairman's prerogative and rule accordingly.

An Amendment need not necessarily substitute words in the Motion, it can simply propose deletions. For instance, taking the example Motion above, somebody might be in favour of a publicity campaign about the profits but not in favour of organised demonstrations. In that case they would move an Amendment to delete all words referring to the demonstrations.

Again, an Amendment might aim not at deleting anything from the Motion, but at adding something to it. For instance the mover of the Amendment might wish to add to the campaign against profits, "that a deputation be sent to the House of Commons to interview the local Member of Parliament about the profits," or it might propose "that a letter of protest be sent to the local press."

COUNTER-AMENDMENT

Now let us consider a simpler Motion and an Amendment which seeks to substitute it as a whole.

The Motion is for example:

"That this meeting calls upon the Government to nationalise the engineering and shipbuilding industry."

There may be somebody in the meeting who is not in favour of nationalisation but in favour of some form of Government action. In that case the Amendment might be moved as follows:

"That this meeting expresses its dissatisfaction with the present methods of management in the engineering and shipbuilding industry and calls upon the Government to set up a public Court of Enquiry to investigate this and to make recommendations for improvement."

It will be seen from this example that the Amendment proposes an entirely different course of action and therefore aims at completely eliminating the Motion. It is therefore known as a *Counter-Amendment*.

PROPOSING A DIRECT NEGATIVE

Somebody who is opposed to nationalisation might attempt to move an Amendment as follows:

"That this meeting is not in favour of the nationalisation of the engineering and shipbuilding industry."

Such an Amendment would not be in order because it is a *Direct Negative* to the Motion and the Chairman would therefore have to refuse it. It is completely unnecessary because the purpose of such a proposed Amendment can be met by simply voting against the Motion.

MOVING AN ADDENDUM

Somebody in the meeting might fully agree with the Motion but think that it needs strengthening by an additional clause. So he moves an *Addendum* as follows:

"At the end of the Motion add the following words, 'and we call upon the Members of Parliament who belong to this union to sponsor a Bill for this purpose'."

When an Addendum has been moved and seconded the Chairman should ask if the mover and seconder of the Motion are agreeable to the Addendum being incorporated in the Motion. If they agree, he should ask if there is anybody in the meeting who objects to this course. If nobody objects then the two propositions are merged and become the Motion.

It is important to note that it is not sufficient for the Chairman to obtain the consent of the mover and seconder of the Motion to have the Addendum merged. There may be somebody in the meeting who wants the Motion to remain in the form in which it was moved, in that case the Chairman is not entitled to merge the Addendum in the motion without a vote on the issue. Therefore after discussion the Chairman would simply call for a vote, "for" or "against" adding it to the Motion.

If the Addendum is defeated the Motion stands as it was, but if it is carried the Chairman should say *"the original Motion as amended now is"* (then read the Motion and Addendum as one).

In this form it is known as the Substantive Motion and is then open to further Amendments.

MOVING A RIDER

A *Rider* is the same as an Addendum in so far that

it seeks to add words to the Motion without any deletion. But there is just a slight difference. Whereas
the Addendum adds words which become an integral
part of the Motion, a Rider adds words which are
simply operative to the Motion. For example the
Motion is:

*"That a Committee be formed to raise a fund for
building a trade union hall in this locality."*

A Rider would be to add the following words:
*"and that a further meeting shall be called to receive
a report within the next three months."*

A Rider is subject to the same procedure as an
Addendum, and if somebody in the above case
objects to another meeting being called within three
months to hear a report, the Chairman must submit
the Rider to the vote to decide whether it shall be
added to the Motion. If the Rider is carried, the
Motion with the addition of the Rider, becomes the
Substantive Motion, and is then open to further
Amendment.

AMENDING AN AMENDMENT

An Amendment which seeks to displace a Motion
entirely is referred to as a Counter-Amendment, and
it may happen that some people in the meeting
neither agree with the Motion nor the Counter-
Amendment, and if they are in the majority they can

vote down both propositions.

But their opposition to the Counter-Amendment may not be an opposition to the main principle of it, but to some minor point, and if this minor point could be amended they would be willing to support this Counter-Amendment.

In that case somebody can move an Amendment to the Amendment; and if it finds a seconder, it will then be open to discussion like an ordinary Amendment.

Now the Chairman cannot permit two Amendments to a Motion to be discussed at the same time. But when he has an Amendment to the Amendment he is confronted with the position of which Amendment is to be put against the Motion. Therefore he puts the Motion on one side whilst the meeting decides which Amendment it prefers. In this case discussion must be confined to the two Amendments and must not make reference to the Motion. Movers of Amendments have no right of reply to discussion.

After the meeting has decided which Amendment it prefers, the Motion is brought forward again and the discussion is resumed on that Amendment and the Motion, and those who have already spoken in the discussion on the two Amendments are entitled to speak again because they are now discussing the merits of the Amendment in relation to the Motion.

AFFIRMING THE MAIN PRINCIPLE

It sometimes happens that time is spent in discussing Amendments to a Motion which is afterwards rejected. If the Chairman is alert he can often visualise that possibility in respect to certain Motions.

For instance, somebody might move a Motion *"That a coach outing for members and wives shall be organised by the committee for June 1 and the venue shall be Blimpton-on-Sea."*

Now it is easy to realise that such a Motion could give rise to a number of Amendments from amongst those who favour an outing. There may be divided opinions on whether it should be train or coach; whether the wives should be included or not; whether the date should be different; and whether the venue should be changed. Much time might be spent in discussing these details only to find out that when the Motion is submitted to the vote the majority are against any outing being organised at all.

To avoid such waste of time the Chairman should suggest, on the ground of expediency, that the main principle, *"that an outing be organised"* should be decided first, and he should invite somebody to move accordingly. After discussion on this straight proposition he should take the vote "for" and "against"

54

If it is defeated, the whole matter is finished without any time being wasted on details. But if the meeting is in favour of the main principle he then returns to the original Motion, and Amendments can then be moved in respect to the details.

Deciding the main principle is not a fixed rule of procedure, but rather a matter of expediency and commonsense on the part of the Chairman which will find a ready response and appreciation from all in the meeting who wish to avoid unnecessary waste of time.

PART III

VOTING

TAKING THE VOTE ON MOTIONS AND AMENDMENTS

ALTHOUGH MOTIONS and Amendments must be read or clearly formulated when they are moved, they should be repeated by the Chairman immediately before voting in order that there shall be no doubt about the terms of the propositions on which the meeting is being asked to make its decision.

If there is an Amendment as well as a Motion before the meeting, the Motion must be read first, then the Amendment. But in taking the vote the Chairman must submit the Amendment first, and take the vote on it "for" and "against".

He does this by saying, *"all those in favour of the Amendment, please show."* Then, *"all those against the Amendment, please show."*

Incompetent Chairman often make the mistake of taking the vote "for" the Amendment, then "for" the Motion. This is quite wrong, because it denies to those who might be opposed to both propositions the opportunity of recording their vote. By this mismanagement on the part of the Chairman they are committed to accepting either one or the other proposition, when in fact they want neither. Therefore, the rule must be observed that the voting on one proposition must be completed "for" and "against", before any vote can be taken on a second proposition.

If there is a majority of votes against the Amendment it is declared lost, and if there are no other Amendments proposed, the Chairman must then submit the Motion to the vote.

If the Amendment that is carried is a Counter-Amendment, however, no vote whatever is taken on the original Motion because it has already been knocked out. The Counter-Amendment having been carried, then becomes the Substantive Motion, and is itself open to further Amendments being proposed providing such Amendments do not seek to re-introduce the principle which was contained in the original Motion that was defeated.

But now let us look at the procedure in regard to Amendments which do not seek to negative the Motion, but only to amend or delete a part of it, or to add something to it.

The same order of voting applies, namely, that the Amendment must be voted on first; and, if defeated, the Motion stands as it was and is then voted on in its original form. But if the Amendment is carried, the procedure is different from the case of a Counter-Amendment, because the original Motion has not been knocked out, but has simply been altered in part. This altered Motion is then referred to by the Chairman either as the "amended Motion" or the "substantive Motion", in order to distinguish it from the original Motion; and in this case, it is necessary to take another vote "for" and "against" the amended, or substantive, Motion.

RESOLUTION

Only after a Motion, or a Substantive Motion, has been carried, is it correct to refer to it as a Resolution; and since this is what the meeting has resolved, it should be recorded in the minutes of the meeting as the Resolution.

VOTING ON AMENDMENT TO AMENDMENT

Now let us look at the voting procedure in the case of an Amendment to an Amendment, referred to previously. To simplify the matter let us refer to these Amendments in the order in which they are moved, as the first Amendment and the second Amendment.

Whilst the issues raised by these two Amendments

are being resolved, the Motion is temporarily put aside. Therefore the first Amendment temporarily occupies the position of the Motion, and after the two Amendments have been discussed the Chairman must take the vote "for" and "against" the second Amendment. If it is defeated, the first Amendment stands as it was and becomes the challenger to the Motion. If, however, the second Amendment is carried that means that the first Amendment has been changed in form, and in that new form becomes the challenger to the Motion. Then the Chairman must pursue the ordinary voting procedure of Amendment versus Motion, as outlined previously.

COUNTING THE VOTES

Unless Standing Orders state to the contrary, it is the usual practice in a small meeting, when voting is by show of hands, for the Chairman to count the votes. But in fairly large meetings, the Chairman is relieved of this task by the appointment of *Tellers,* whose job begins and ends with the counting and reporting of the votes.

The minimum number of Tellers is two and as the Chairman calls for the votes they do the counting. One acts as a check upon the other and their recording should be the same. If they find that their count-

ing is different then obviously one of them has
made a mistake and they must count again until
they agree.

The record of those voting in favour of the proposition which is in front of the meeting is quietly
reported to the Chairman (or minute secretary) who
notes it down on a piece of paper before he calls for
the votes against. Then the same process takes place
on the votes against. The Chairman must then read
out to the meeting the figures of voting and declare
the proposition carried or lost, as the case may be.
It is not sufficient for him to announce the result
without stating the figures.

When the meeting is voting on propositions which
have aroused a very strong division of opinion the
Tellers are selected equally from the opposing sides.
They can either be nominated by the meeting or
chosen by the Chairman and assented to by the meeting. In a very large meeting there may be four or
more (always an even number) of Tellers, acting in
pairs (one from each opposing side) and taking the
count in sections.

In an ordinary meeting with show of hands voting,
the Tellers are themselves entitled to vote unless
there is a Standing Order to the contrary. But if they
exercise their right to vote they must do so at the
time the other votes are being counted. They can-

not add their votes after the Chairman has received the results.

VOTING AT LARGE MEETINGS

In large meetings like the Trades Union Congress, another method of voting is by voice. The Chairman says "All those in favour shout 'aye'." Then "All those against shout 'no'." According to the volume of voice for the "Ayes" and "Noes" the Chairman declares the proposition carried or lost. This is a time-saving method of voting and is quite suitable in a large meeting when there is an overwhelming opinion for or against the proposition, but not when the opinion is fairly evenly divided. In the latter case, the Chairman must either use the show of hands method, or in the case of a conference of affiliated organisations, the method of "block" voting. The block vote method means that the delegates hold up a card which represents the number of votes which his organisation is entitled to cast on the basis of the number of affiliated members.

When the voting on a proposition shows a very narrow majority for or against, anybody on the defeated side is entitled to challenge the vote if he thinks a mistake has been made in the counting. In that event the Chairman must take the vote again, and the second vote stands as the decision of the meeting.

THE CHAIRMAN'S VOTE

In organisations which have Standing Orders or rules governing meetings, it is usual for the position of the Chairman to be defined in respect to voting rights. In such cases those orders or rules must be complied with. But in other cases the following practice operates.

At an ordinary public meeting the Chairman is not entitled to a vote unless the voting for and against a proposition is even, in which case he is entitled to what is known as a *Casting Vote*. This means that having announced the result of the voting as even, he can then announce that he intends to add his Casting Vote for or against the proposition, which will accordingly entitle him to declare the proposition carried or lost as the case may be.

This practice also applies in the meetings of an organisation where a *permanent* Chairman officiates. But when a Chairman is *temporarily* appointed from a gathering of delegates or members he is entitled to two votes: one his *personal* vote as a delegate or member; and the other, his Casting Vote as a Chairman. He is not bound to use his personal vote, however; and his Casting Vote as Chairman can only be used if the voting of the meeting is even. Moreover, he cannot cast two votes together by reserving his personal vote and declaring it at the same time as he gives his Casting Vote. If he wishes to use his personal vote he must do so at the time the votes are being counted, otherwise he forfeits it on that issue.

At first sight this might not appear to be important. But if we look at it in practice it will be seen that it can have a *very* important effect upon the result. Supposing, for example, the vote on a Motion is even; thirty for and thirty against. If the Chairman favours the Motion he can then give his Casting Vote which entitles him to declare the Motion carried. But if the voting was twenty-nine for and thirty against without the Chairman having cast his personal vote, he would not then be able to use either his personal vote or his Casting Vote; and he would have to declare the Motion lost.

The Chairman, whether permanent or temporary, is not compelled to use his Casting Vote; he may prefer to remain neutral. But since a Motion cannot be left undecided, the Chairman must, if he declines to use his Casting Vote, declare the Motion lost, or in other words defeated.

VOTING IN ELECTIONS

TRADE UNIONS and most other organisations have their own rules governing the methods for election of their officers; and these are too varied and involved to be dealt with here. But there are many meetings where the election of delegates, deputations or committees,. are not prescribed for by special rules. In such cases there is a general practice for such elections.

NOMINATIONS

First, let us take the case where one delegate is to be elected. The Chairman calls for nominations from the meeting. Those present are entitled to call out the name of a candidate, and in strict procedure this nomination must be seconded before it can be accepted by the Chairman. The value of insisting upon a seconder lies in the fact that if no seconder is forthcoming that is evidence that the candidate has no support in the meeting beyond the one person who nominated him, and therefore it would be a waste of time to submit his name to the vote. As nominations are called out and seconded the Chairman (or secretary) should write them down in the order in which they are called.

When more than the required number of nominations have been called out, anybody who has not made a nomination, or is not himself a candidate, is entitled to move "That nominations close." The Chairman must accept that motion and put it to the meeting without any discussion. He can test the meeting by asking for a formal acclamation of "agreed", but if anybody dissents he must submit the motion to a vote. If it is carried it closes nominations; if it is lost the Chairman must take further nominations. When he feels that the meeting has exhausted its nominations he should formally ask if the meeting agrees that nominations close, and if it does, he proceeds to the next stage of the election.

VOTING ON NOMINATIONS

If one delegate is to be elected and only one candidate has been put up, the Chairman can declare that candidate elected without submitting his name to a vote. This is quite in order because the meeting, having already decided to send a delegate must carry out that decision, and if there is only one candidate it obviously follows that he must be the delegate. But the delegate might prefer to know by a decisive vote that he has the support of the meeting, and, if he feels that way, he can request the Chairman to formally take a vote. But if the Chairman accedes to this request he does so purely as an act of courtesy to the delegate.

When more than one delegate is required and the number of candidates nominated does not exceed the number of vacancies to be filled, the Chairman can in this case also declare the candidates elected without taking a vote. But if he chooses to use his prerogative and take a vote, he must do so in a purely formal manner by saying to the meeting, "are you all in favour of these candidates being our delegates?" and the meeting usually assents by calling "agreed" In other words, he submits the names collectively to the meeting for approval, and should not submit them separately as individuals, because that would make a contest of the election when there is, in fact, no basis for contest.

If, however, when nominations are closed, the number of candidates exceeds the number of vacancies, the Chairman must submit all the names separately to the vote, but before doing so he must read the list of candidates to the meeting.

In submitting the names of the candidates to the vote there are two methods which are commonly used. One is to take the names in the order in which they are written down, the other is to start with the name at the top of the list and then the name at the bottom, thereby working from top and bottom to the centre until the last name is reached in the centre of the list. Whichever method is used rests with the Chairman, but it is always advisable for him to announce to the meeting, before he starts to take the vote, which method he will pursue.

He must only take an affirmative vote on each

candidate. No vote against the candidate is needed because the votes which are given for candidate B, are in effect votes against candidate A.

In the simple method of election the candidate who has the highest number of votes is declared elected; and similarly if more than one delegate is required, those candidates, up to the required number, who receive the highest votes are declared elected.

It is important to remember, however, that in an election where more than one delegate is required, each member of the meeting is entitled to as many votes as the number of delegates to be elected. In other words, if two delegates are required, each person in the meeting is entitled to two votes; the two votes cannot be cast for the same candidate, but must be divided between the two candidates of his choice. The same principle applies if more than two delegates are required, i.e., four delegates, four votes each voter.

Although a voter is not *compelled* to cast all his votes, he nevertheless is *expected* to do so; otherwise he is not fully participating in the decision of the meeting to elect a number of delegates. For example, to take an extreme case, if everybody cast only one vote and they were all for the same candidate, it would vitiate the previous decision of the meeting to send more than one delegate.

When voters are entitled to more than one vote it is most important that the Chairman should inform the meeting of this before he commences to take the vote, because failure to remind the voters of this right can easily give rise to confusion when the vote is being taken and necessitate starting again.

When voting on two candidates in a list is equal, it is necessary to submit those two names to the vote again in order to decide which one is elected, and this time each voter has only one vote.

For example, two delegates are to be elected, and there are sixty people at the meeting each entitled to two votes which makes a total of 120 votes to be given. Candidate A receives forty votes, B receives thirty, C receives thirty and D receives twenty. Therefore candidate D is defeated but candidates B and C must be submitted to the vote again, with every voter having only one vote, to decide which of these two candidates is chosen as delegate.

CLEAR MAJORITY VOTE

The method of election in which the candidate simply has to obtain more votes than the next highest can be termed the *Simple Majority* method. But there is another method in which the candidate must obtain a clear majority over the combined votes of his opponents. This can be called the *Clear Majority* method. This is regarded as a fairer method and more decisive. It is a method which is often used when electing somebody to a certain office which he will have to fulfill over a period of time. In such a case it is desirable that the election should show that this person has the confidence of not less than 50 per cent of the members who vote. This is achieved by taking a second vote on the two candidates who have received the highest votes, if neither of them has a clear majority over the combined votes of the others.

Example: One hundred voters are present at the meeting and there are four candidates for one office. To obtain a clear majority over all his opponents the successful candidate must therefore obtain not less than fifty-one votes. But when the vote is taken on the candidates A, B, C, and D, it might show the following results: A thirty-five votes, B thirty, C twenty-five, D ten. Since candidate A has not received sufficient votes to indicate that he has the confidence of a clear majority of the voters, the two candidates with the lowest votes drop out, and a second vote is taken on the two highest. Those who voted for the defeated candidates must now decide which of the two remaining candidates they prefer. In the second voting everybody is entitled to vote again, and the candidate who now receives the highest number is declared elected. In such an election it sometimes happens that the candidate who was second highest in the first voting secures the highest votes in the second voting, but the result of the second vote is the decisive one.

THE EXHAUSTIVE VOTE

In the election of committees a more complicated method of voting is sometimes used, known as the *Exhaustive Vote*. It takes much longer than the two methods described above and it is usually confusing in a general meeting. Therefore it should only be recommended for use at meetings where the voters are experienced and have a knowledge of the Exhaustive Vote method. However, let us consider it.

In this method of election several rounds of separate voting might have to be taken according to the number of the candidates nominated.

Example: A committee of five members is to be elected and there are eight candidates. Each member in the meeting would be entitled to as many votes as amount to one less than the number of candidates, therefore in this case they would have seven votes to cast in the first round of the election, for seven of the candidates. The candidate who receives the lowest number of votes then drops out of the election. That leaves seven candidates for five seats.

So a second round of voting takes place with each voter now using six votes. Again the lowest candidate drops out and the third round takes place, each voter using five votes this time. The five candidates who receive the highest votes in this third round would be declared elected.

It can readily be seen that the larger the number of candidates in excess of the number required, the more the number of rounds of voting increases in order to carry through the process of elimination. And though ardent advocates of procedure contend that this is the fairest method of election, which may be quite true, it can easily be tedious and confusing. For most practical purposes the Simple Majority or the Clear Majority methods are quite suitable and satisfactory.

PART IV

DIFFERENT KINDS OF MEETINGS

TRADE UNION BRANCH MEETINGS

THE PROCEDURE for branch meetings of all our trade unions is very similar in character. In general the Agenda includes the following items in this order:

1. Minutes.
2. Correspondence.
3. Financial Report.
4. Enrolment of New Members
5. Delegates' Reports.
6. Election of Delegates to Local Committees or Conferences.
7. Ballots for Officers.
8. Lecture by Visiting Speaker.
9. Any Other Competent Business.

Much depends on the Chairman as to whether the business is carried through in an interesting or dull manner. He should not be satisfied with simply getting through the business, he should conduct it in such a way as to hold the attention of the members and thereby encourage them to attend the branch regularly.

The following methods in dealing with the various items on the Agenda should prove effective.

MINUTES

After the Chairman has called the members to order and declared the meeting open, his first item of business is the *Minutes* of the previous meeting. It is the usual practice for the Minute Secretary to read these but they can be read by the Chairman himself if he prefers this practice. But whoever reads them should do so standing, not sitting. By standing, the reader commands better attention from the meeting and an upright position improves the voice delivery. If they are read in a sitting position the tendency of the reader is to bend over the table, head down, with the result that it becomes difficult for everyone in the meeting to hear him distinctly.

When the Minutes of the meeting have been read the Chairman must ask the meeting for a formal Motion *"that they be accepted as a correct record."* If somebody in the meeting wishes to challenge the correctness of the Minutes he must do so at that moment and the Chairman must give him the right to state precisely in what respect he considers the Minutes are not correct.

If the error indicated by the challenger is admitted by the Secretary and the Chairman, there is no need to submit an Amendment to the meeting on it, but if it is disputed the challenger must then move an Amendment that the Minutes be rectified in accordance with his stated objection. The Amendment must be seconded by some other member in the meeting and then the Chairman can allow a limited discussion on it.

In voting on the Amendment the Chairman should rule that only those who were present at the meeting covered by the Minutes are entitled to vote. This is a necessary safeguard to prevent absentees, who may not like the decisions which were taken, from interfering with the records of the meeting.

If the Amendment to rectify the Minutes is carried by a majority of those who were present at the meeting, the correction should immediately be inserted in the Minute book and initialled by the Chairman. To facilitate such corrections it is advisable that when writing the Minutes, a suitable margin should be left down one side of the page which can be used for inserting any corrections or omissions.

When the Minutes have to be altered, the formal Motion for passing them should be changed to read *"That the Minutes as amended be accepted as a correct record."*

After the Minutes are passed the Chairman must append his signature and the date.

CORRESPONDENCE

Unless it is the practice for the branch secretary to read the *Correspondence* it should be read by the Chairman, not by the Minute Secretary. This leaves the Minute Secretary free to devote himself to his job of writing a correct record of the proceedings. He can then note the item of Correspondence as it is being read and give full attention to minuting the discussion and decisions which may follow.

Correspondence is an important feature in trade union branch business and the reading of it should be done efficiently. Read it standing, not sitting. Don't mumble through it. Don't read it in a dull monotonous voice and don't gabble on as though all sentences run into each other without punctuation. Such reading can be very irritating to the listeners and cause loss of interest in the subject.

It should be read clearly and intelligently, with proper pause and emphasis where needed. This stimulates interest and prepares the members for discussion.

It is important that the Correspondence should be sorted by the Chairman at the beginning of the meeting and placed in its proper order, so that if there are several items of Correspondence dealing with the same subject they can be read together before they are discussed.

In some trade union branches the practice is to read the whole of the Correspondence right through before asking for discussion and decisions. In other branches the practice is to read and discuss each item separately.

If you wish to do the job thoroughly the latter course is the best, because the contents of the letter are fresh in the minds of the members when they are asked for discussion. Further, it can save time because it obviates the necessity to read the letter again—a request which is often made when the former course is adopted.

Not all Correspondence requires discussion, some of it is simply information. In such cases the Chairman can quickly pass on to the next item by formally asking the meeting to agree that the letter be noted as information.

The Chairman must use his own judgment on whether a letter calls for discussion. If he thinks it does, he should give a lead to the meeting by saying: "What are your views on that subject, Brothers?" or "Does any Brother wish to say something on this?"

The Chairman must use his discretion on the time to be spent on each item. When he thinks the views of the members have been adequately stated, and no benefit can be obtained from further discussion, he should announce that he intends to close the discussion after the next speaker. If there are several members still rising to speak, he can say: "I will take two (or three) more speakers." He will generally find that the meeting will approve of his decision. A good Chairman knows when to intervene with such a ruling without creating the impression that he is stifling discussion. Members appreciate a Chairman who stops unnecessary discussion and prevents waste of time.

Some items of Correspondence are related to other subjects on the Agenda and should therefore be reserved for reading when those subjects are reached. For instance, a letter of information or request from the Trades Council is best read when you reach the subject of Trades Council delegate's report.

ENROLLING NEW MEMBERS

The method of enrolling new members varies according to the rules of the Union, but the historic practice of "reading in" new members still prevails in many unions, especially in the old-established craft unions. It is indeed a very good practice, because if it is well done it impresses upon the candidate the importance of the step which he is taking.

Unions have their own "Initiation Address' which is read to the candidate by the Chairman. The procedure which operates in many of the unions is as follows. The candidate must be proposed and seconded by established members of the branch who vouch for his qualifications as a workman and his general worthiness to become a member of the union. The Chairman then asks if any member has any reasons to offer why the candidate should not be admitted into membership. All this takes place whilst the candidate waits outside the room. If the branch agrees to accept the candidate the Chairman then calls for the sponsors to bring him into the room. He is directed to the Chairman's table and stands facing the Chairman. The Chairman then calls for every one present to stand whilst he reads the "Initiation Address". At the end of the "Address" the Chairman shakes hands with the candidate and declares him a member of the union. The members show their approval by applause and the candidate takes a seat amongst them, and the branch passes on to next business.

Much depends upon the Chairman to make this ceremony dignified and impressive so that the candidate experiences a sense of pride and responsibility in becoming a member of the union. The "Initiation Address" is the most important part of the ceremony and it should be read clearly and distinctly so that its principles are impressed upon the candidate and renewed in the minds of the members present. The Chairman must insist upon complete silence whilst the "Address" is being read so that the full importance of the occasion is conveyed to the candidate.

DELEGATES' REPORTS

When the delegates to the District Committee of the union, the Trades Council, local Labour Party or any special conference, are called upon to give their *Reports* the Chairman should invite them to come to the table to do so. This is much better than the delegate giving his Report from the body of the meeting. If the delegate gives his Report standing at the Chairman's table it provides the following advantages: it adds a greater sense of importance to the Report; it enables the speaker to face his audience instead of addressing the back of their heads; the audience, who always like to see the person who is speaking, can do so with comfort if he is in front of them; the speaker has the advantage of a table which he can use for his notes and so avoid fumbling with them in his hands; and it assists the Chairman to quietly notify the speaker when he is reaching his time limit.

Before the delegate begins his Report the Chairman should inform him of the time at his disposal.

The Chairman must insist upon silence whilst the Report is being given and no interruptions should be permitted. If any member attempts to raise a question or make an interjection whilst the Report is being given, the Chairman must firmly rule him out of order and insist that the delegate shall finish his Report before anybody else is allowed to speak. This is most essential otherwise the delegate will be drawn into replying to points raised before his Report is completed, and general confusion will arise.

Immediately the delegate finishes his Report the Chairman should ask if somebody will formally move *"that the Report be accepted"*. This in effect means that the meeting recognises that the delegate has carried out the duty entrusted to him. When that Motion has been formally agreed to by the meeting, the Chairman should then declare that the Report is now open to questions and discussion. He should then rule that questions will be taken first. If, during the question time, someone starts to make a statement on the Report or to propose a course of action in connection with it, the Chairman must promptly interrupt him and ask him to reserve his remarks until after the questions have been dealt with with.

The delegate can either answer each question as it arises or make a note of them and answer them all together. If the delegate chooses the latter course the Chairman should announce that fact to the meeting. After the questions have been asked and answered, the Chairman should announce that he will now take discussion. It is then in order for any member to rise and speak about the Report or to propose a Motion arising from its contents.

There may be a hesitancy to start discussion so the Chairman should always prepare to meet this situation by noting the important points in the Report whilst the delegate is speaking and then, if he finds it necessary, he can give a lead to the discussion by mentioning the points on which he thinks the meeting should express an opinion.

At the end of the discussion the delegate has the right to reply, but he need not do so unless he thinks it necessary to clear up certain impressions or doubts. No further discussion can be allowed after the delegate has replied.

If, in the course of general discussion, somebody proposes a Motion in relation to some portion of the Report and the Motion is seconded and discussed, the delegate, if he desires, can participate in the discussion on the Motion the same as any other member, but he has no special rights in this respect and

81

his contribution does not close the discussion. In this case the person who moves the Motion has the right to reply and to close the discussion on that Motion only.

If there has been no discussion except on the Motion, the delegate has no right to reply after the Motion has been voted on. But if there has been discussion of a general nature on some other aspects of the Report, then the delegate is entitled to reply to this, but he is not entitled to use this right to express opinions in opposition to the decision which has already been recorded.

After the Motions have been disposed of and the general discussion has been closed by the reply of the delegate, the Chairman should formally ask the meeting for a Motion *"that the Report be approved,"* and by general assent that closes this item of business.

Before passing on to the next item on the Agenda, the Chairman may, by way of courtesy, ask for a vote of thanks to the delegate. It can be done very quickly and it encourages the delegate to know that his services are appreciated by the members.

ELECTION OF DELEGATES

If there is an item on the Agenda for the election of delegates to Trades Council, local Labour Party or any special local Conference the Chairman should reserve the correspondence dealing with that subject and read it when that item is reached, thereby giving a suitable introduction to the election.

If it is a special conference to which delegates are invited the correspondence will give the particulars about the date, place and time of the conference.

But if it is a formal notice for delegates to Trades Council, local Labour Party or some standing committee with which the branch is connected, these particulars might not be given, on the assumption that the branch is already acquainted with them. This assumption may be correct in regard to the officials, but the ordinary member might not know. Therefore, in this case, the Chairman, before calling for nomination of delegates, should state the particulars of when, where, and how often the delegates will be expected to attend. Those who are nominated will then understand the obligations involved and know whether they are able to fulfil them.

If there is a hesitancy on the part of members to accept nomination, a few words from the Chairman on the importance of the branch being represented will often overcome this hesitancy and awaken the members to a sense of duty to the organisation.

It frequently happens that members who are nominated decline to accept because of other commitments, and there are members in the room who would accept, but because they are lesser-known members they are not nominated. This position can be tested if there are no accepted nominations by the Chairman asking if there are any *Volunteers*. If there are, he should name the Volunteers and then ask if somebody will formally nominate them. If the number of Volunteers does not exceed the number of delegates required the Chairman should then ask the meeting to agree formally that the nominees be accepted as the delegates. This procedure of nominating the Volunteer and securing the endorsement of the branch puts him in order and gives him proper authority as a delegate. Strictly speaking, unless this is done, he is not a delegate and cannot be entered in the Minutes as such. Also, if there are more Volunteers than delegates required the procedure outlined puts the matter in order for a vote to decide who is to be eliminated.

LECTURE BY VISITING SPEAKER

Most trade union branches invite speakers from time to time from other organisations to address them on some special subject which is of interest to the members. This helps to make the branch meetings more interesting and encourages the members to attend. It has an educational value, stimulates the exchange of ideas and encourages wider activity.

The preliminary arrangements for engaging speakers are attended to by the Branch Secretary or perhaps a special lecture secretary. He should, in his correspondence to the *Visiting Speaker* give full details of the time and place of meeting and inform him of the time allocated for his speech, and the time allowed for questions and discussion. It is essential for the Speaker to know in advance how long he is allowed for speaking so that he can prepare his speech or lecture accordingly. It is unfair to the Speaker to let him prepare for an hour's speech and then to discover when he arrives at the meeting that he only has twenty minutes.

If the branch opens at 7.30 p.m. and the Speaker will not be called upon to begin his lecture until 8.30 p.m. he should be informed of that by the secretary in his correspondence, so that he does not arrive too early and have to wait whilst routine business is cleared.

A Visiting Speaker is entitled to expect the branch to make proper arrangements to ensure a good attendance. It is unfair to invite a Speaker to give up his evening to attend the branch and perhaps make a long journey for it, without taking steps to see that he is rewarded with a good audience. Therefore, unless special summons notices are to be issued to the members, the date of the meeting should be so arranged as to allow time for announcements of the lecture to be made in at least two preceding branch meetings. In addition to this, it is always advisable to get the word round to leading union members in the workshops, such as shop stewards, so that they can use their influence to encourage members to attend.

In many trade union branches, members come into the meeting to pay their contributions, and after doing so, some of them leave when there is no business being dealt with which specially attracts them. Therefore on the evening of the lecture, the Chairman should announce early in the proceedings that a speaker is coming and urge the members to remain. Another effective method of holding the members is to hang a large notice in front of the Chairman's table announcing the lecture and the name of the Speaker; and this is convenient for any members who arrive late. Such a notice can easily be prepared before the meeting opens. A large sheet of white paper (placard size if possible) and a blue pencil or crayon is all that is necessary.

After the secretary has attended to the preliminary arrangements the duties of the Chairman are important in relation the Visiting Speaker. He should see that a vacant chair is reserved at his table for the

Speaker and when he arrives he should not be left standing at the back of the room wondering what to do. The doorkeeper or some other branch officer should inform the Chairman, and he should promptly announce that the Speaker has arrived and invite him to come to the vacant seat at the table. If there is still some branch business to dispose of before the lecture begins, the presence of the Speaker at the Chairman's table encourages the members to remain in the meeting.

When the Speaker comes to the table the Chairman should shake hands with him and make him feel welcome.

Before the Chairman introduces the Speaker he should exchange a few words with him about the procedure and time allowed and ask the Speaker if there is any special point that he wants mentioned in the introduction. It is usual for the title of the lecture to be arranged beforehand in correspondence and the Chairman should confirm this with the Speaker. If the Speaker intends to use notes or quote from documents the Chairman should see that a space is made available on the table for him.

Introductory remarks by the Chairman are important, but they should be very brief. It is very bad grace, and impolite to the Speaker, for the Chairman to start expounding his own views on the subject of the lecture before calling upon the Speaker. I once remember listening to a Chairman doing this at such length that when the Speaker was finally called upon, he looked at his watch, put away his notes, rose to his feet and said, "Well, you have listened to a very interesting lecture, now are there any questions?"— and sat down, much to the embarrassment of the Chairman. In the circumstances, that very adroit and cutting remark met with the general approval of the meeting, and the lecturer, having a journey to make and indicating the lateness of the hour, took his departure. How long it took the Chairman to live down that mistake I don't know, but I'm certain that he learned two salutary lessons on Chairmanship; first, to clear the other business and keep to the time appointed with the Speaker; and second, to make a brief introduction for the Speaker and avoid trespassing on his subject.

In introducing the Speaker, the Chairman should state the Speaker's name, the organisation with which he is connected, the official position which he occupies in that organisation, if any, and the subject which he will speak about. If he is a well-known person with an outstanding record in public life, reference should be made to this briefly but in a way that will uphold his prestige and give him the feeling of being properly introduced.

At the end of the lecture the Chairman should ask for questions to the Speaker on the subject of his address. If somebody attempts to raise a question which has no relationship to the address he should be ruled out of order.

After questions have been dealt with it is usual to invite discussion, and here again the Chairman should rule out of order any person who attempts to introduce irrelevant matters into the discussion. At the end of the discussion the Chairman should offer the Speaker the opportunity of replying to the discussion if he desires to do so. After this, the Chairman should call for a vote of thanks to the Speaker and invite somebody to move and second a Motion to that effect. This can either be done formally or by short appropriate remarks from the mover and seconder, and then, without any further discussion, the Chairman should ask the meeting to show approval by acclamation and hand-clapping.

The Chairman should then shake hands with the Speaker and personally thank him for his visit and enquire whether there are any fares and expenses to be met. If there are, he should either call the secretary to the table or direct the Speaker to the secretary, so that the account can be settled. Avoid putting the Speaker in the uncomfortable position of having to ask for his expenses. Many Speakers have been victims of negligence in this matter by the Chairman and secretary and have left the meeting out-of-pocket, rather than be put in the undignified position of asking for the expenses that are due to them.

The whole proceedings in connection with a Visiting Speaker should be so conducted by the Chairman that the visitor is not only made to feel welcome, but that he is also able to leave the meeting with an impression of an organisation that is well-conducted and efficiently administered by its branch officers.

OTHER BUSINESS

The last item on the branch agenda is usually *Other Business.* It is the item under which members are permitted to raise matters which are not otherwise provided for in the Agenda. It can become a very disconcerting item unless it is well-managed by the Chairman.

The time allowed for this item at the end of the meeting is usually between five and ten minutes. Therefore, if several members unexpectedly raise controversial matters and the meeting is allowed to enter into general discussion the proceedings can become very protracted. When that happens, members generally begin to drift out of the meeting and it breaks up in an unsatisfactory way. This is a situation which the Chairman must always endeavour to avoid.

Therefore when the Chairman calls for Other Business he must exercise his authority to prevent long introductory speeches on the matters which the members raise. On any matter which is likely to arouse controversy, and which is not imperative to have settled at the meeting, the Chairman should rule that it be placed on the Agenda for the next meeting. Chairmen often get caught unawares on the number of items raised under Other Business, and this results in the closing time of the meeting being extended. He can avoid this position by adopting the following practice. At a convenient moment in the earlier proceedings of the meeting he should ask if there are any members who wish to raise matters under Other Business when that item is reached. He can ask them to name the subject that they intend to raise, and then, in accordance with the number and nature of the subjects indicated, he can use his judgement as to whether he should make adjustments in his timetable. If this practice is adopted, the members will become accustomed to it and be ready on request to name the subjects that they wish to raise. The Chairman should take the names of these members and when he reaches Other Business he should call upon them by name in the order in which they were recorded. Further, under this practice the Chairman is entitled to rule out any member from raising new matters in Other Business if he has not already indicated his intention to do so. By the above practice, Other Business is prevented from being a vague, unestimated item on the Agenda, dragging on long after the meeting is due to close.

Under Other Business the moving of Motions is permitted unless there are Standing Orders which state to the contrary. But the Chairman must exercise his judgement on this. If the Motion proposed is one which can be moved and seconded without provoking opposition and lengthy discussion he should permit it, but if it is otherwise he should rule that it be tabled as a Notice of Motion for the next meeting. It is obviously unwise to permit an involved debate to commence in the last few minutes before the meeting is due to close. If, however, the meeting shows a desire to clear the issue up right away, a limited extension of time should first be agreed to. But even so, it is a very undesirable procedure for highly controversial Motions to be sprung on the meeting in the last few minutes before closing time. Such Motions should be notified to the Chairman before Other Business is reached so that they can either be dealt with as a special item on the Agenda of that meeting or reserved for the following meeting according to the wishes of the members.

After the Chairman has disposed of Other Business he should rise to his feet and make any final announcements that are necessary. If he has a few minutes in hand he can make a few closing remarks about the business that has been transacted and then terminate the proceedings in a proper manner, by striking his bell or gavel and saying "*I declare the meeting closed.*"

COMMITTEE MEETINGS

THE TWO FORMS of committee most commonly in use in trade union and other working-class organisations are *Standing Committees* and *Special Committees*

The functions of a Standing Committee, which is a permanent body elected for administrative purposes within the rules of the organistion are in almost every case laid down in the rules of the organisation; and sometimes, though more rarely, the procedure for conducting the meeting is laid down in the form of Standing Orders.

A Special Committee (sometimes referred to as a *Sub-Committee* or an *Ad Hoc Committee*), is set up temporarily for a special purpose; and therefore, when it has carried out that purpose, it disbands. Being a temporary body, it is less likely to have

Standing Orders, but the special purpose for which it is set up must be defined by the meeting which created it. This definition is known as the *"Terms of Reference"* of the Committee. Since the Resolution appointing the Special Committee will usually have stated the purpose of the Committee, this is taken as the Terms of Reference. For example, the Resolution may be: *"That a Special Committee be formed to prepare a scheme for rendering financial aid to our aged and retired members and to report its findings to our next monthly meeting."* Here the Terms of Reference are quite clear and the Committee would have to confine its functions to those terms.

GENERAL PROCEDURE

At Standing Committee and Special Committee meetings the general procedure for transacting business (unless Standing Orders are to the contrary) can be summarised as follows:

At a Standing Committee an Agenda is generally necessary and Minutes must be taken. Also there must be a rule on the number of members needed in attendance to "form a *Quorum*". If less than the stipulated Quorum are in attendance the meeting cannot be held; no decision can be taken, nor will any discussion be minuted since it will be informal. It is usual for the Agenda of a Standing Committee to have as its first item "Apologies for Absence"; which are either conveyed to the meeting verbally by one of the members present, or read out by the Chairman.

Special Committees do not usually need to have an Agenda because there is only one item for discussion, and only in exceptional circumstances is it necessary to have a rule laying down a Quorum. Also, unless the committee is to hold several meetings, it is not necessary to compile Minutes. *It is necessary, however, for somebody to be appointed to take notes of the proceedings,* in order to prepare a report to the main body which appointed the committee.

The *Rules of Debate* which apply in a General meeting are *not* operated in Committee meetings. Discussion can take place without having a definite Motion on the table; and it is more usual for Motions to be proposed at the end of discussion, not at the beginning. Committee members are permitted to speak as often as they feel necessary providing they do not do so to the exclusion of others. In speaking, it is not necessary for them to stand, they can do so seated. When Motions and Amendments are proposed in Committee it is not necessary for the mover to find a seconder.

The *Chairman* of a Committee has the same right

to participate in discussion and to voice his opinion on a Motion as any other Committee member. If he is one of the elected Committee members who has been appointed to the chair by his colleagues he has the same right as they have to vote, i.e., he can exercise a Personal Vote. But he is *not* entitled to a Casting Vote in addition unless the rules of the organisation or the Standing Orders of the Committee have granted that right (see pp. 62-3).

EX-OFFICIO COMMITTEE MEMBERS

It frequently happens that the constitution of a Committee provides for the Chairman and Secretary of the main body to attend the Committee meetings although they were not elected to the Committee. When that is the case they attend *ex-officio,* i.e., by virtue of their office. Such *ex-officio* members have the right to participate in discussion but *not* to vote, because strictly speaking they are not members of the Committee. But in cases where the constitution of an organisation declares that its Chairman should be the *ex-officio* Chairman of a particular Committee, then it usually follows that although he has no Personal Vote he is entitled to exercise a Casting Vote in the event of an even division on any proposition.

CO-OPTION OF MEMBERS

Sometimes when a Special Committee is appointed the parent body grants it powers to bring into its meeting additional persons, having a specialised knowledge of the subject to be decided. Such persons are known as *Co-opted Members.* They attend in a purely advisory capacity; and though they may be granted full rights to participate in discussion, they cannot be granted any right to vote.

REPORTING BY COMMITTEE

Committees are usually expected to submit reports on their work to the parent body either verbally or in written form. Standing Committees make periodical reports but Special Committees usually issue only one report covering the subject for which they were appointed.

Reports of Standing Committees are based upon majority rule, and if there is a minority opinion in such a Committee it is not the practice to report that opinion. The minority is expected to abide by, and give support to, the majority decision.

But in the case of Special Committees the practice is different. Here, the minority opinion is not submerged, and where such a division of opinion exists it is the practice to make known to the parent body the opinion of the majority and the minority, and to leave that body to decide which opinion it accepts. In cases where a written report has to be submitted, and where there is a strong division of opinion in the Committee, two reports can be issued—a Majority Report and a Minority Report, each being signed by the respective supporters.

DATE OF MEETING

Standing Committees usually have fixed dates for their meetings, but Special Committees arrange their own dates. Therefore, when more than one meeting of the Special Committee is required the Chairman or Secretary of the Committee must see that the date of the next meeting is fixed before the Committee adjourns.

PUBLIC MEETINGS

THERE ARE various forms of public indoor meetings which in the main can be described under the following headings:

1. For demonstration and propaganda purposes only.

2. For publicity and recruitment of new members to an organisation.

3. For public protest against the action of a certain authority.

4. For obtaining public opinion by resolution in support of a certain project.

5. For the purpose of reporting on a certain event.

The reader will realise that there are distinct differences between these various kinds of meetings; and that therefore, the preparations, arrangements and management of the meetings also varies. The committee or organisation responsible for the meeting must prepare accordingly.

PREPARATION FOR THE MEETING

Taking them in the numbered order mentioned above let us consider the characteristic features of each meeting.

Number 1. Specially attractive publicity intended to appeal to the widest section of possible supporters. Large hall, colourfully decorated. Popular speakers who have the ability of arousing strong enthusiasm amongst an audience. Inspiring music and song provided by orchestra or choir. Special attention to the stewarding of the meeting with adequate number of stewards to control crowds, to take tickets at doors, and to assist the Chairman in taking money collections. Arrangements should be made for supplies of literature and special sales stewards. At such a meeting no questions or discussion would be allowed.

Number 2. Special publicity efforts amongst those particular sections of people whom it is intended to recruit. For example, if it is a union meeting to recruit engineering workers then special efforts should be made, in addition to public notices in the local press and on the hoardings, to make the meeting known in the local engineering factories through printed leaflets distributed amongst the work-people by union members; by chalk notices at the factory gates; by contacting shop stewards and urging them to use their influence to rally the workers to attend the meeting. The speakers at the meeting should be fully qualified to speak about the work and policy of the particular organisation, and should in the main confine their remarks to that subject. There should be a plentiful supply of recruiting leaflets and membership forms, and for the benefit of those who do not fill up a form at the meeting the Chairman, in his closing remarks, should clearly indicate where and how such persons can make local contact with the organisation after they have reflected on the meeting and read the literature which has been given to them.

Number 3. In this case the publicity would focus attention on the grievance about which the protest meeting was being held. The speakers would build their speeches around that grievance and the audience would be asked to express support to the protest in the form of a resolution. It might elect a deputation to interview the Authority in question. It might decide on lines of activity for broadening and developing the campaign of protest until the grievance is remedied. If a deputation is to be elected a list of suitable names for recommendation to the meeting should be prepared, and other nominations left open to the meeting.

Number 4. At a meeting which is called to support a certain project like the "launching" of a new organisation or the organising of some special event, the publicity would centre around the objective. Well-known names of sponsors should be collected and advertised. They should be invited to sit on the platform although they might not be speaking at the meeting. The speakers should specially explain the project in view and what it is expected to achieve. A resolution should be drafted and submitted to the meeting for approval, and arrangements made to collect names and addresses of intending members and supporters. Provision might be made for questions and discussion from the audience.

Number 5. Reporting a special event such as a Congress, or the visit of a delegation to another country, makes a special appeal to studious-minded persons, therefore the publicity material should prominently refer to the event which is to be reported at the meeting. The speakers should be persons who have been connected with the event and who can therefore give a first-hand report of it. If there is more than one speaker they should, previous to the meeting, arrange their notes so that each speaker deals with separate aspects of the subject. At such a meeting as this it is absolutely essential that time be allowed for questions from the audience and replies by the speakers.

PROCEDURE AND CHAIRMANSHIP

Having broadly outlined the varying features of the different kinds of public meetings, now let us consider the general procedure which should apply to all of them, and some of the essential points in connection with the Chairman's duties.

First, a word about the meeting hall. The committee responsible for arranging the meeting should first make a rough estimation of how many people they expect to attract to the meeting, based upon the public interest in the subject of the meeting, the extent of the publicity campaign to be undertaken, and the attracting value of the speakers. They then have a reasonable idea of the size of the hall required. It is a mistake for them to book a large hall unless they feel confident about filling it. One hundred people in a hall which only holds one hundred, is a success, but two hundred people in a hall which holds eight hundred is a failure. The psychological effect on an audience where the hall is full is very important. It stimulates a feeling of strength, whereas a hall only half full has a depressing effect upon both the audience and the speakers.

But of course, it is possible for a committee to overestimate the attendance, and find on the night of the meeting, that not sufficient people turn up to fill the hall.

In this situation certain steps should be taken to minimise the effect of the poor attendance. First, if there is gallery in the hall, close that, and use only the ground floor. The people on the floor are not likely to notice an empty gallery. Secondly, try to get the audience in a compact position. Don't encourage the people as they arrive to stray into any isolated seat, have stewards to guide them to seats near to one another. Thirdly, if the seats are divided into a centre section and two sides, fill up the centre section first to within a few rows of the back, before starting to use the sides. A compact body of people in the centre block of seats, looking straight before them at the platform—over rows of filled seats—will hardly notice the empty side seats, or those empty behind them. Always fill the front centre seats. The sight of empty seats depresses an audience and discourages a speaker.

If representatives from the press have been invited to the meeting, or are expected to come as a result of the publicity, have a press table available for them near the platform to make it easier for them to take notes.

The Chairman and committee responsible for the meeting should be in attendance at the hall at least fifteen minutes before the starting time, so that they can meet—in an ante-room if possible—to review final details.

Speakers should also be present early and the Chairman should discuss the time-table of the meeting with them and any points he wants them to note about procedure, before they go on to the platform.

Some speakers—especially those who use carefully prepared notes—have a preference for either left or right of the Chairman's table, and the Chairman should ascertain this before-hand and try to accommodate that speaker in order to place him at his ease.

If it is a large platform, the committee and close supporters should be arranged as a platform party, to occupy seats behind the Chairman and speakers. A well-filled platform is much more impressive than an empty space.

Attention to the order of entry on to the platform

is important. The Chairman should lead, the speakers should follow in their order of importance, and then the committee and supporters. On the Chairman's table there should be a bell or mallet and a water jug and glass. If there is a microphone it should be tested before the meeting opens to see that it is already switched on and is in working order. It is most disconcerting for the Chairman to start speaking into a dead "mike" and having to halt whilst somebody scurries around trying to get the apparatus to work.

When the platform party goes on, all of them, including the Chairman, should take their seats. The Chairman should then give the audience a few moments to settle down before he rings his bell or bangs his mallet to call for silence. He should then rise to his feet to make his opening statement, which should cover the objects of the meeting, the naming of the speakers and any reference to the meeting procedure on which he thinks the audience should be informed, such as whether time will be allowed for questions and discussion.

The Chairman's remarks should be terse and to the point. At a public meeting people come to hear the speakers, not the Chairman. He may be a more fluent speaker than the advertised speakers, but an audience always expects the Chairman to act as master of the ceremonies and not to play the part of a star performer. When the Chairman finishes his opening remarks he should then announce his first speaker. He should introduce him with a few appropriate remarks about his qualifications and his record of service in public life or whatever field of work he specialises in. Such remarks—commonly called a "build-up"—confirms the prestige of the speaker and prepares the audience for attentive listening.

The Chairman should have his time-table in front of him and he should quietly notify the speaker when he is nearing the time limit. This can be done by the Chairman touching his bell or passing a note to the speaker three or five minutes before his time expires. The arrangement to do this should have been made with the speaker before he goes on the platform so that the speaker knows what to expect. The bell, as a signal, is less distracting to the speaker than the passing of a note. If the note method is used only two words in block capitals should be written, i.e., "THREE MINUTES". This notice can be read at a glance and gives the speaker time to make his closing remarks.

When the speaker sits down, the Chairman should not immediately rise to his feet, he should allow a few moments for applause. When the applause has ended he should then rise to make his next announcement. If there are more speakers to be heard he should announce them in turn with appropriate personal words of introduction. Although a speaker may be well-known, it is a mistake at public meetings for the Chairman to simply say, *"Our next speaker is so well-known that he needs no words of introduction from me."* The Chairman must not assume that everybody in the audience is as fully informed about the speaker's qualifications and record as he is himself. There may be many people present who only know the speaker by name and they will appreciate a proper introduction from the Chairman, providing it is short and to the point. Also, the words of introduction from the Chairman provides the audience with a few minutes necessary interval—or breathing space—between the two speakers.

Further, when the Chairman has important announcements to make to the audience, he can effectively use the interval between the speakers to do so. It is a mistake to save important announcements for the very end of the meeting. When people are about to leave they are not so attentive to further remarks from the platform. Most regular meeting-goers have experienced occasions when these last-minute announcements have been shouted from the platform, above the noise of shuffling feet and conversation, as the audience is leaving the hall —and they know how ineffective such announcements are. It is the kind of untidy ending to the meeting which the Chairman should always avoid.

LITERATURE

Many Chairmen make that mistake in connection with literature. The sale of literature at public meetings is an important item and the Chairman can greatly assist this by devoting a few minutes to the subject in between the speakers. He should have copies of the literature on his table which he thinks the audience should be specially encouraged to purchase. He should briefly mention the importance of this literature and state the title and the price. If this announcement can be followed by a few minutes interval between speakers, to allow the literature stewards to go down the gangways to make sales amongst the audience it usually has good results. Those who do not obtain the literature because they are not seated conveniently near the steward, will look for their opportunity to obtain it as they leave the hall. By the Chairman making an announcement about the literature, it gives authority to the sales—encourages the audience to buy, greatly helps the stewards to sell, and gives them a standing of importance to which they are entitled. If the Chairman makes no announcement, the audience streams out at the end of the meeting, with the less experienced meeting-goers regarding the literature stewards at the doorway almost as persons committing a nuisance.

INTERRUPTIONS

During the proceedings of the meeting the Chairman is responsible for maintaining good order amongst the audience. Serious interruptions very seldom occur at working-class meetings but when they do, if it is an organised attempt to break up the meeting and the Chairman is unable to stop it, he must rely upon the hall stewards to eject the interruptors. At public meetings it is always advisable to have stewards available for that purpose.

In the case of less serious interruptions a good Chairman can usually quell any disturbance. He has the advantage of his authority as Chairman and can, in almost every case, depend upon the support of the audience in checking interrupters.

Often, when interruptions take place they are provoked by some remark in the speaker's address, to which somebody in the audience objects. This is where the sense of judgement on the part of the Chairman must be exercised. If the interruption is no more than a single ejaculation the Chairman need not intervene. Usually the speaker, if he is quick-witted, will answer the remark of the interrupter in the next few sentences of his speech and if he does it well he will generally silence him. But if such interruptions are repeated, or if the interrupter rises to his feet and attempts to make a statement, the Chairman must deal with him. He should ask the speaker to stop for a few moments and resume his seat, whilst he rises to his feet to rebuke the inter-rupter. He should point out to the offender that he cannot permit such interruptions, that it is unfair to the speaker and to the audience who want to listen. The Chairman, by associating the audience with his ruling, rallies their support, strengthens his own authority and psychologically isolates and over-whelms the interrupter.

Another very effective method is for the speaker or Chairman to score with a quick humorous retort at the expense of the interrupter, thereby making him the object of laughter from the audience. This can be even more effective than the first method because it destroys the dignity of the interrupter. But the retort must not be ponderous—it must be spontaneous, quick and very pointed to be effective, and not every speaker or Chairman is tempera-mentally fitted for that.

RESOLUTIONS

At a public meeting where a Resolution is to be submitted for endorsement by the audience, the best practice is for the Chairman to read the Resolution at the end of his opening remarks and to call upon the first speaker to act as the mover and the next to act as seconder. If there are more speakers they act as supporters. At the end of the last speech—before the Chairman makes his closing remarks—the Resolution should be submitted to the vote of the meeting either by acclamation or by show of hands.

The committee responsible for the meeting may have decided that in addition to the platform speakers, discussion on the Resolution should be allowed from the audience for a limited period. Before asking for the first speaker from the audience, the Chairman should state the time which will be allowed for general discussion and then ask those in the audience who wish to speak to indicate by holding up their hands. That enables the Chairman to decide how much time he can allow to each speaker. If the total time for discussion is half an hour and six persons want to speak, he can allow them five minutes each. If, however, there are thirty or more would-be speakers the Chairman should rule that that number is not practical, and he should then fix a limit that he thinks is suitable and select the speakers in the order in which they rise and catch his eye. If he selects several speakers one after another who all speak for or against the Resolution, he should then ask if anyone wishes to express the opposite point of view, and if there is, he should give him preference to speak next.

In cases where provision has been made on the time-table of the meeting for discussion from the audience, it is necessary to make provision also for a short reply to the discussion by the first platform speaker who moved the Resolution, and immediately following this reply the Resolution should be submitted to the vote of the meeting.

VOTE OF THANKS

Often at public meetings, provision is made by the Chairman for votes of thanks to the speaker to be moved just before the close of the meeting. Especially is this done in the case of speakers who have travelled from outside the locality to the meeting, or if they are guest speakers from another organisation. It is a form of courtesy which makes a friendly conclusion to the meeting.

Often at small meetings, votes of thanks are moved without previous arrangement, but at larger public meetings—and if the Chairman intends to call for votes of thanks—it is advisable for him to arrange before the meeting who is to be the mover and the seconder. This enables them to reflect upon a few suitable remarks and prevents some garrulous enthusiast jumping to the occasion and making an unnecessarily long statement.

Movers and seconders of votes of thanks must be very brief in their remarks—not longer than five minutes for the mover and three minutes for the seconder. They must not introduce new contentious matter in their remarks. They can refer to some of the points made by the speaker and express appreciation for his address and for the service which he has rendered. No discussion can be allowed by the Chairman on votes of thanks. After the usual applause from the audience to indicate support to the Motion, the Chairman should invite the speaker to make a brief reply.

CLOSING THE MEETING

The closing of the meeting is important from the stand-point of the impression left on the audience. The Chairman must aim at holding the attention of the Audience to the very last moment. He should rise to his feet for final remarks. These remarks should be brief and should refer to the outstanding purpose for which the meeting was organised. He should call upon the audience to bear in mind the speeches they have heard. If proposals for action have been put forward, the Chairman should briefly reiterate these and call upon the audience to go away determined to follow up these proposals. He should aim at terminating the meeting on a high note of enthusiasm. At the end of his closing remarks he should not just stop and leave the audience wondering whether there is anything more to wait for, he should definitely terminate the proceedings by saying, *"I now declare this meeting closed."*

PUBLIC DEBATES

PUBLIC DEBATES have a procedure which is quite distinct from that of an ordinary public meeting. At a debate the platform speakers are verbal opponents conducting a controversy before an audience and each endeavouring to convince the audience that his point of view is correct and the other one is wrong.

Usually only two speakers take part in a debate, but it is possible to have more and in that case they would be known as supporters to the two principals.

Any controversial matter can be made the subject of debate, but it should always be presented in the form of a Motion. It should also be in the positive —not in the negative form. For example. *"That Socialism is the only permanent solution to unem-*

ployment. . . ." *"That the British prison system is in need of reform. . . ."* *"That the present expenditure on the Armed Forces is against the national interest."*

Care should be taken in drafting the proposition which is to be debated, so that the point at issue is clearly evident, not only to the platform opponents, but also to the audience. For example, the following proposition is not clear, *"That nationalisation is not advisable."* One might very well ask, nationalisation of what? and for whom is it not advisable? Surely it would be better to state the proposition in the following terms, *"That nationalisation of industry is a failure,"* or *"That nationalisation of industry is in the best interests of the nation."*

For a debate there must be at least two speakers and a Chairman. If it is a debate organised by an established debating society the rules of that society will prescribe the procedure to be followed. But if it is a public debate arranged by individuals or by organisations other than debating societies, the procedure will have to be specially formulated and mutually agreed between the parties concerned.

The person who is to speak in favour of the proposition is known as the Opener, and he must speak first. The other one is known as the Opposer. The usual procedure is for each speaker to speak twice for an equal period of time and then for the Opener to close the debate with a few minutes' reply. The second period for each speaker would be shorter than the first.

If the meeting were to last two hours the arrangements would be something like the following:

Chairman's introductory remarks ...	8 minutes
Opener in debate	30 ,,
Opposer ,, ,, ...	30 ,,
Second speech	
Opener ,, ,, ...	15 ,,
Opposer ,, ,, ...	15 ,,
Closing reply	
Opener ,, ,, ...	7 ,,
Submitting Motion to vote of audience	3 ,,
Chairman's closing remarks ...	7 ,,

If votes of thanks were to be moved to the speakers, which is the usual custom in debates, about five minutes could be allowed for that before the closing remarks of the Chairman and that would make the above time-table exactly two hours.

The Chairman in opening the proceedings should welcome the audience, remark on the importance of the subject to be debated, introduce the speakers and refer to their qualifications, state the procedure laid down for the debate, read the Motion for debate and then call on the Opener to speak. The Chairman is not entitled at any time during the proceedings to express his personal opinion for or against the Motion under debate, and he must be strictly impartial in his treatment of the speakers.

In addition to opening and closing the meeting the principal duty of the Chairman at a debate is to maintain order and see that the speakers do not exceed their allotted times.

Strict enforcement of the time limit for the speakers is absolutely essential in a debate. If the Chairman allows one of the speakers to exceed his allotted time he is acting unfairly to the other speaker and will almost certainly provoke protests from the speaker against whom he is offending and from his supporters in the audience. At a debate, both the speakers and the audience keep a check on the time, and any infringement is quickly noticed.

Before the debate opens, the Chairman should arrange with the speakers the signal which he will use when they are approaching their time limit. He should touch his bell or tap the table with his mallet two minutes before the limit is reached, as a warning that the speaker has that time in which to finish his speech. It is very important that the Chairman should explain in his opening remarks to the audience the signal arrangement which he will use, so that they also understand that the first signal is a time limit warning, and not a signal for the speaker to sit down. Failure to explain this might lead to protests from persons in the audience who have been closely watching the time.

When the two minutes' warning expires the Chairman must promptly give his second signal and that must be obeyed immediately, by the speaker resuming his seat. If the speaker continues to speak after the second signal the Chairman must rise to his feet and insist that the speaker sits down. Appeals from the speaker for "just a few more moments" must be firmly rejected by the Chairman.

The first speaker should carefully prepare his opening speech to cover the allotted time. But the Opposer should not prepare his first speech to cover the full time because, in addition to stating his case on the subject, he is, in fact, replying to the Opener and he should therefore leave himself time to answer some of the principal points made in the opening statement.

The second speeches of the contestants can be planned beforehand to bring out new weighty arguments, but in the main, the time should be used by each to demolish the case of the other.

Unless otherwise mutually decided, the Opener has the right to make a short closing statement. He therefore has an advantage over his opponent and the Opposer should remember this and try to avoid making statements in his second speech which the Opener can score from in his final remarks.

Immediately the final remarks of the Opener have been concluded the Chairman, without any further comment, must read the Motion again and submit it to the vote of the meeting. He then accordingly declares who is the winner in the debate.

If a vote of thanks is moved it should include both speakers but only the winner of the debate is entitled to reply. If the loser has made a good show the Chairman can, merely as an act of courtesy, invite him also to reply to the vote of thanks, but he is not entitled to claim it as a right.

When the speaker is replying to the vote of thanks it is courtesy for him to refer to the efficient and impartial manner in which the Chairman has conducted the proceedings and to ask the audience to express their appreciation to the Chairman by including him in the vote of thanks.

After the applause, the Chairman should then close the meeting with a few suitable remarks.

OUTDOOR MEETINGS

OUTDOOR MEETINGS are mainly organised for propaganda or protest purposes. There are two principal forms of such meetings, namely the street corner meeting where the audience is chiefly collected from passers-by, and the one which is an organised assembly, referred to as a demonstration, which takes the form of the crowd converging on the meeting place individually or in organised procession.

STREET CORNER MEETING

Let us first consider the procedure at the *Street Corner Meeting*. The platform is usually a small folding rostrum, a chair or a box, upon which only one person can stand at a time.

The chief function of the Chairman is to attract the audience and then hand the meeting over to the speaker. There is a technique about collecting "the crowd". The essential thing is to arouse curiosity amongst passers-by sufficient to cause them to stop to find out what the meeting is about. Unless a body of supporters are already assembled round the platform, the Chairman must rely upon building his audience one by one as people come along. This often means that when he first gets up on the platform he must be prepared to talk to an open space. The tendency is—unless he is well-experienced in such meetings—for him to shout loudly in an effort to make himself heard by persons whom he sees in the distance. In so doing he discourages them from coming close to the platform to find out what is going on, because they can hear all about it from a distance. In other words he is abating the curiosity which might draw them close enough to form a crowd. If they stop at all they remain at a distance and after a few moments, not feeling that they are part of the meeting, they wander away.

If the Chairman at a Street Corner Meeting will remember that he depends upon curiosity to collect his crowd he will not speak loudly, but quietly, so that the people have to come closer to hear what he is saying. Having come closer they feel that they are part of the meeting and are more likely to stay.

Often when a Street Corner Meeting is started there are half a dozen supporters already present, including the speaker and literature sellers. When the Chairman opens up, these supporters should not stand behind him but should get in front and form the nucleus of a crowd. Strangers are much more likely to come to the platform if they see others there. The stranger is reluctant to stand in front of the platform alone because he hesitates to make himself conspicuous.

A very effective method of drawing a crowd is for one of the supporters to interrupt the Chairman with questions or remarks which create the impression of opposition. It is a development of the curiosity trick which seldom fails to draw others in. The average person finds it difficult to resist listening to an argument between two or more persons and quite unconsciously he helps to form the crowd which the Chairman requires to make a meeting.

I remember a street-corner speaker in the days of mass unemployment who had a novel method of arousing curiosity for attracting a crowd to start his meeting. He would attract attention by simply rolling up a newspaper in the shape of a torch, setting fire to it and holding it in front of him whilst it burnt out. He would sometimes burn half a dozen newspapers one after the other without saying a word. Passers-by attracted by the strange spectacle would come closer to watch, then, when he had his crowd, he would say: "You saw me burn those newspapers, well I did so because they are hiding the truth from the people and I want to tell you about that." Having heightened their curiosity he would begin to address them about social conditions and accuse the newspaper editors of refusing to publish the facts. He charged them with deceiving their readers, but all this was only part of his introductory remarks, and as he talked on the crowd forgot about the newspapers and became interested in his general arguments about social conditions, whilst newcomers helped to swell the crowd to a successful gathering. That was a simple form of showmanship which usually achieved its purpose because the average person is naturally curious.

I am not advising this method, I am simply quoting it to impress upon the Chairmen of Street Corner Meetings that they must bear in mind the part which curiosity plays in gathering an audience.

When the Chairman has collected his crowd he should announce the speaker and give him the usual build-up about ability and qualifications. At this stage he should ask the audience to close in to the platform so that the speaker does not have to strain his voice unnecessarily, and so that they can hear more distinctly what he has to say. People in a compact audience are less likely to stray away from the meeting. The Chairman, having done his job, then steps down and makes way for the speaker. From then on the speaker must depend upon his own ability to hold the crowd and secure an attentive hearing. If there are interruptions he must deal with them himself. He cannot keep stepping down to let the Chairman call for order.

Of course, if the interruptions are persistent and the speaker is unable to proceed with his address, the Chairman should ask the speaker to make way for him to appeal to the crowd. He should then appeal to their sense of fair play and inform them that if they will quietly listen to the speech they will be given the opportunity of putting their questions to the speaker as soon as he has finished. Unless it is an organised opposition, such an appeal from the Chairman—with the promise of questions—seldom fails to produce the desired results. The Chairman then steps down and the speaker resumes his address from where he left off.

When the speaker finishes, he should step down from the platform and the Chairman should then take over again for a few minutes to make any announcements necessary about literature and collection. He should then, without undue delay, call for questions to the speaker. When the first question is put, the Chairman should repeat it so that everybody in the audience can hear, and then immediately call upon the speaker to mount the platform to reply.

If there is a hesitancy in the audience to start the questions the Chairman should give them encouragement by reminding them of some of the principal points in the speech and thereby help to give them ideas for questions. If he still has difficulty in getting the first question he can turn to one of his known supporters and say: "I have noticed that you listened very attentively to what the speaker had to say. Surely there is some point on which you would like further information?"

This prompting should produce a response from the supporter in the form of a question which might even have the appearance of challenging something which the speaker had said. The audience, in most cases, will think the questioner is one of them, and once the questions have been started they will lose their hesitancy and will follow up.

At a Street Corner Meeting it is not necessary for the subsequent questions to be put through the Chairman. They can be put direct to the speaker. The first question is put through the Chairman, but when the speaker has answered that he should remain on the platform and ask for the next question direct. Otherwise it means that the Chairman and speaker have to change over twice with each question, and that introduces a break in the proceedings and affords an opportunity to some of the audience to leave the meeting. To retain a standing audience in the open it is essential to hold their attention all the time.

Before the speaker replies to a question he should repeat it to the audience, because often those who are standing behind the questioner are unable to hear what he is saying. If some of the audience do not know what the speaker is replying to they will lose interest in the meeting and leave.

In replying to questions the speaker should make his reply to the crowd. He should not answer direct to the questioner because that will encourage him to interrupt the reply and result in a personal argument that will disturb the order of the proceedings.

Hecklers frequently crop up at Street Corner Meetings and often, without realising what they are doing, they turn a sparsely attended meeting into a mass gathering by the attention which they arouse from passers-by. The experienced Street Corner Speaker is not upset by their appearance—he welcomes them as a magnet for his crowd and a target for his wit.

It is most important when dealing with a Heckler for the speaker not to lose his temper. An irate speaker will lose the sympathy of the audience and play into the hands of the Heckler. If the speaker remains calm he will generally find that after a short time the crowd will turn on the Heckler and insist that he remains quiet or gets out of the meeting so that they can listen to the speaker without interruption.

Of course, the speaker who is clever at repartee can often make quick, humorous retorts to the Heckler which makes him the object of laughter from the crowd and drives him away from the meeting feeling very small. That is the most effective way of dealing with the Heckler.

When the time arrives for closing the meeting the

speaker must step down and hand the meeting over to the Chairman. Before stepping down he should announce that the Chairman has something to say before the meeting closes. This helps to hold the crowd so that the Chairman can make his final remarks and formally declare the meeting closed.

OUTDOOR DEMONSTRATIONS

Now a few words about *Outdoor Demonstrations*. Usually it is now the practice for loudspeaker apparatus to be used at these meetings. Many public speakers make the mistake of speaking too close to the microphone. This has the effect of distorting the reproduction through the loudspeakers and, although they produce a loud noise, their words are blurred and indistinct, with the result that the audience find it difficult to follow what they are saying.

The crooner can hug the "mike" with satisfactory results because he is pouring into it a slow, treacly murmur, but speech—especially platform speeches—is a series of staccato utterances which reverberate on the microphone if the speaker is too close. Therefore if the speaker will remember just before he begins that he is not a crooner, he will do the right thing and stand back from the "mike" so that the audience gets a more perfect reproduction of his words. About twelve to eighteen inches away, according to the volume of the apparatus, is generally suitable for open-air speaking. If the speaker watches his audience he will know whether those at the back are able to hear him without any strain.

Frequently at Open-air Demonstrations the Committee responsible wishes to have a Resolution submitted. In this case the normal procedure in respect to Motions and Rules of Debate is dispensed with. The Resolution has already been formulated by the Committee and the Demonstration is simply asked to express its approval of that Resolution. No questions, discussion or Amendments are called for. The Chairman should read the Resolution at the beginning of the meeting and again at the end, before he submits it to the vote of the crowd. He should take the vote "for" and "against" the Resolution by a show of hands or acclamation. If he takes it by show of hands he does not require to count the vote, he simply declares it carried or lost according to the visible strength of voting.

CONFERENCES

A *Conference* is an assembly of delegates called together by a special committee or an established organisation, for the express purpose of discussion and decision. It may last one or more days and its procedure is generally much more complicated than that of a Public meeting. Therefore, a Conference is not the place for a novice to be in the chair. It requires a Chairman of experience who has a sound knowledge of the Rules of Debate.

In a Public meeting the audience is there mainly to listen to what is said without actively participating in the proceedings, but at a Conference everybody present has the responsibility of taking part in discussion and arriving at decisions. A Chairman who is not capable can cause serious confusion in a Conference, especially if the Agenda is a complicated and detailed one which involves alterations to the rules and constitution of the organisation concerned.

In addition to the ordinary Rules of Debate the Chairman must be fully conversant with any special rules which have been laid down for the conduct of business.

SPECIAL COMMITTEE

When a Conference is to be held, the organisation responsible for it usually appoints a Special Committee to attend to the arrangements and details. These will include the booking of the hall; the issuing of notices calling for delegates; the selection of stewards and doorkeepers; the seating accommodation and platform arrangements; invitations and facilities for Press representatives, and the printing of material necessary for the delegates.

The conduct of the proceedings is usually worked out by the Executive Committee of the organisation. This will involve the drafting of the Agenda and time-table; the formulation of Resolutions to be submitted; the selection of movers and seconders for Resolutions in the name of the Executive; the procedure for submitting Amendments; and the nomination of any Committees or Commissions which are considered necessary for operation during the Conference.

RESOLUTIONS

At a Conference the propositions for discussion which are printed on the agenda are nearly always under the title of Resolutions, not Motions. This is because they have already been discussed and resolved by the Executive Committee or one of the lower units of the organisation and are being submitted to the Conference for approval or rejection. If Amendments have been sent in for the agenda, they of course appear under that title against the appropriate Resolution.

CREDENTIALS

For Conferences, delegates must be issued with a

special *Credential.* This should contain a perforated section on which the particulars of the delegate can be written or typed in. This section is given to the door steward by the delegate as he enters the Conference hall so that the organisation has a record of the delegates in attendance.

It is most essential that all stewards should be present at the hall before the doors are opened. They must see that every door is covered by one or more stewards, otherwise they will not be able to properly check the delegates' Credentials and prevent unauthorised persons from gaining admission.

CREDENTIALS COMMITTEE

It is necessary to have a small committee known as a *Credentials Committee,* whose duty is to collect the Credential slips from the door stewards and compile a report on attendance and representation for presentation to the Conference before it closes.

STANDING ORDERS COMMITTEE

At a Conference where there are numerous Resolutions and Amendments, it is essential to have a Special Committee which acts in an advisory capacity to the Chairman. It considers the Amendments to Resolutions and when, as frequently happens, two or more Amendments are similar in character, it interviews the delegates who are to move these Amendments, and either secures the withdrawal of the unnecessary repetitive Amendments or arranges for them to be coalesced into one composite Amendment. They also arrange which of the delegates concerned is to move and second such Amendment. In accordance with the changes which they are able to arrange they make proposals for adjusting the time-table for various items. Such committees are known under various titles, including *Standing Orders Committee, General Purposes Committee* and *Resolutions Committee*. They must of course keep the Chairman closely informed of any changes which they make, and this is usually done by one of the Committee submitting a factual report to the Conference on each separate item on the Agenda before it is reached by the Chairman. The Conference can either approve of the Committee's report or reject it. If it approves, the necessary adjustment in procedure is made by the Chairman. If it rejects the report the Committee must take the proposals back for reconsideration. But only in very exceptional circumstances does the Conference reject the Committee's proposals, because if the delegates most closely concerned do not object, the others feel that they have no grounds to do so.

At political party Conferences there might have to

be Special Commissions set up to function during the Conference on various aspects of policy about which statements have to be drawn up and submitted to the Conference.

The operation of Committees during the Conference therefore makes it necessary for those who are responsible for the preparation of the Conference to engage a hall which has suitable Committee rooms attached.

CHAIRING A CONFERENCE

At Conferences of more than one day's duration arrangements are sometimes made for different Chairmen to preside at each session. But the Chairman-in-chief is the one who opens the Conference and in the final session he takes over again and closes it.

In a Conference, the Chairman is always expected to deliver an opening address. This might be either an individual address or one which has previously been vetted by a Committee and is intended to express the collective opinion of that Committee. Which form it takes depends upon the rules of the organisation. In any case, only the Chairman of the opening session delivers an address. Any other Chairman who presides at subsequent sessions formally opens the session without a speech.

CONFERENCE PROCEDURE

The general rules and procedure for dealing with Resolutions, Amendments and other motions have already been considered and these apply in a Conference, except where rules of procedure drawn up by the organisation or Conference Committee state otherwise.

There are, however, a few special points that need mentioning here. First, on the question of speakers.

It is often claimed that the fairest method of selecting speakers from the floor of the hall is for the Chairman to point to the one who springs to his feet first and catches the Chairman's eye. But this claim is a very disputable one on a number of grounds. Firstly, if a large number of delegates in different parts of the hall are clamouring to speak it is difficult for the Chairman to decide who is the first. Secondly, the Chairman, although he is expected to be impartial in his choice, can quite easily avoid choosing a particular delegate whom he wants to exclude from discussion because he knows him to be a critic. Thirdly, the quiet type of delegate is not so likely to compel attention from the Chairman as the noisy and aggressive one. Fourthly, the choice of speakers at random can result in a disproportionate selection in respect to representation or point of view.

Choosing the next speaker on the principle of catching the Chairman's eye may be a suitable method in a small Conference where unfairness can be more easily checked, but in a large Conference other methods are generally more satisfactory.

The alternative methods are: (1) That the names of speakers should be sent up to the Chairman written on a slip of paper and that the Chairman should call upon them in the order in which the names are received. (2) That the slips of paper containing the names of would-be speakers should be sent to the platform and that a small Committee should collect these and submit them in the form of a list for the Chairman to call upon. In both methods we must depend upon the Chairman or Committee to be unbiased in naming the speakers.

The Conference always likes to know the names and particulars of those who take part in discussion. Therefore if the method of catching-the-Chairman's-eye is used in choosing speakers, the delegate who gets the floor should, before he commences to speak, announce his name, organisation, branch, or district that he is representing.

When the name-on-the-slip method is used the Chairman is able to call upon the delegate by name and announce any other particulars which have been supplied. With this method it is a good practice for the Chairman to announce two speakers—the one who is about to speak and the one who is to follow. This enables the following-up speaker to be prepared for his call.

In a small Conference, delegates can speak from their place in the hall, but at a large Conference it is much better for them to go to the platform so that everybody can see and hear them more clearly. Usually a rostrum is arranged for this purpose, which is at the side or in front of the platform, but a little lower. When the Chairman announces the name of the speaker in advance, it gives him notice to leave his seat and make his way forward to the rostrum in readiness for his call.

When a rostrum is used, the best method for signalling the time-limit to the speaker is by the use of electric lights fixed to the rostrum. The Chairman controls these from his table and when the speaker has two minutes to go the Chairman switches on a green light for a moment. When the two minutes are up he switches on a red light which means that the speaker must stop. The Conference is able to see these lights as well as the speaker and if the speaker ignores the Chairman's signal the Conference will quickly indicate its disapproval by calling "Chair", until the speaker stops.

CLOSING A CONFERENCE

A final word about the closing of a Conference. The spirit in which it terminates its proceedings is very important and the responsibility for this rests with the Chairman. In the last session he must see to it that all officials and Committee members who are expected to be on the platform are in their places.

The Chairman is expected to make the final speech to the Conference. He should do so in the form of a summing-up on the work of the Conference and an exhortation to the delegates to follow up their decisions when they get back to their branches and districts.

He must hold the attention of the delegates to the very end and when he rises to make his closing speech he must aim at bringing the Conference to an end on a note of enthusiasm.

The delegates should not rise from their seats until he finally announces: *"I declare this Conference closed."*

INDEX

Bold type indicates the pages on which can be found brief definitions of terms used.

i

INDEX

INDEX

iii

INDEX